P9-CKX-905

DATE DUE

DEMCO 38-296

GREAT WRITERS OF THE ENGLISH LANGUAGE

Nineteenth-Century British Writers

Riverside Community College
Library
4800 Magnolia Avenue
Riverside, California 92506

PR 85 G66 1989
Great writers of the English
language

TAFF CREDITS

Executive Editor
Reg Wright

Series Editor
Sue Lyon

Editors
Jude Welton
Sylvia Goulding

Deputy Editors
Alice Peebles
Theresa Donaghey

Features Editors
Geraldine McCaughrean
Emma Foa
Ian Chilvers

Art Editors
Kate Sprawson
Jonathan Alden
Helen James

Designers
Simon Wilder
Frank Landamore

Senior Picture Researchers
Julia Hanson
Vanessa Fletcher
Georgina Barker

Picture Clerk
Vanessa Cawley

Production Controllers
Judy Binning
Tom Helsby

Editorial Secretaries
Fiona Bowser
Sylvia Osborne

Managing Editor
Alan Ross

Editorial Consultant
Maggi McCormick

Publishing Manager
Robert Paulley

Reference Edition Published 1989
Published by Marshall Cavendish Corporation
147 West Merrick Road
Freeport, Long Island
N.Y. 11520

Typeset by Litho Link Ltd., Welshpool
Printed and Bound in Italy by
L.E.G.O. S.p.a. Vicenza

All rights reserved. No part of this book may be
reproduced or utilized in any form or by any means
electronic or mechanical including photocopying,
recording, or by an information storage and retrieval
system, without permission from the copyright holder.

©Marshall Cavendish Limited MCMLXXXVII
MCMLXXXIX

LIBRARY OF CONGRESS
Library of Congress Cataloging-in-Publication Data
Great Writers of the English Language
    p. cm.
    Includes index vol.
    ISBN 1-85435-000-5 (set): $399.95
    1. English literature — History and criticism. 2. English
literature — Stories, plots, etc. 3. American literature — History
and criticism. 4. American literature — Stories, plots, etc.
5. Authors. English — Biography. 6. Authors. American — Biography.
I. Marshall Cavendish Corporation.
PR85.G66 1989
820'.9 – dc19   88-21077
                                          CIP

ISBN 1–85435–000–5 (set)
ISBN 1–85435–002–1 (vol)

GREAT WRITERS OF THE ENGLISH LANGUAGE

Nineteenth-Century British Writers

William Thackeray

Anthony Trollope

Oscar Wilde

Samuel Butler

MARSHALL CAVENDISH · NEW YORK · TORONTO · LONDON · SYDNEY

Riverside Community College
Library
4800 Magnolia Avenue
Riverside, California 92506

CONTENTS

WILLIAM THACKERAY

1811-1863

F. Stone: William Makepeace Thackeray/National Portrait Gallery, London

William Makepeace Thackeray wrote some of the finest
satirical novels in the English language. And his ebullient
personality matched his most colourful creations. His own life
was as chequered as any work of fiction. Intimate with the
fashionable world, sucked into its unsavoury undertow, he rose
above it to become a grand old man of letters. When he died of
an overstrained heart, the greatest writers of his day lamented,
for he told 'the truth in spite of himself'.

Larger than Life

The public image of the young Thackeray – gambler and rake – concealed a man with a generous heart. Private tragedy was to transform him into a devoted father and man of letters.

Thackeray's life reads like a novel – a Thackeray novel. It was propelled by sudden changes of fortune, none more significant than that following the publication of *Vanity Fair* in 1847. It was his greatest work, and the only English novel of the time to rival Tolstoy's *War and Peace*. At the age of 36, it brought him immense and immediate literary and social success and status. But it did not make his fortune. And having lost his inheritance through gambling and a banking crisis, he spent the rest of his life striving to regain his fortune through writing.

William Makepeace Thackeray was born in India on 18 July 1811, the only son of Richmond Thackeray, a wealthy official of the East India Company, and his 18 year-old wife, Anne. Living in Calcutta, in a mansion serviced by a large staff, the first few years of Thackeray's life were luxurious and exotic: he later recalled his visions of 'great saloons and people dancing in them, enormous idols and fireworks, riders on elephants or in gigs, and fogs clearing away and pagodas appearing over the trees'.

This sort of lifestyle was not to last. One day, his father invited a colleague, Henry Carmichael-Smyth, to dinner – unaware that Henry was his wife's ex-lover. Three years earlier, in England, the couple had been separated by Anne's devious grandmother. She had told Anne that Henry had died of fever, and then packed her off to India. Henry and Anne could not conceal their feelings from each other or from

Richmond. When Richmond died three years later, young Thackeray was sent to school in England, and the following year his mother became Mrs Carmichael-Smyth. Thackeray never saw India again.

From 1817, he attended a private school in Southampton – 'a school of which our deluded parents had heard a favourable report, but which was governed by a horrible little tyrant'. For six year-old Thackeray, it meant dreadful food, beatings, cold – and nightly prayers that 'I may dream of my mother'. His mother returned to England with her new husband in 1820: Thackeray recalled their emotional reunion some 30 years later when he wrote of Henry Esmond's meeting with his mother: "The soul of the boy was full of love, and he had longed . . . for someone on whom he could bestow it."

At the age of ten, 'a pretty, gentle, and rather timid boy', Thackeray entered one of the most prestigious public (private) schools in England – Charterhouse. Despite its reputation, the teaching was poor, and hazing and beating were normal practice. In one particularly unpleasant incident, some senior boys arranged an entertainment in which Thackeray had to fight another pupil. His nose was shattered, disfiguring him for life. Paradoxically, when Thackeray was older, he spoke well of Charterhouse and its system – which he thought had an improving effect. But for Thackeray the schoolboy, Charterhouse deserved a harsher name: he called it 'Slaughter House'.

An only child
(above) For three years, young William enjoyed the retinue of a prince and the undivided attention of his parents. This portrait of Anne, Richmond and their child was made by Calcutta's most renowned artist.

Exotic early years
(left) Though his memories of India were scanty, they were powerful. Thackeray 'could just remember' his late father – along with 'crocodiles floating on the Ganges'.

'Slaughter House'
(right) Thackeray began his 'education as a gentleman' at Charterhouse in 1822.

National Portrait Gallery, London

Private Collection

A threatened future
(above) Young Thackeray had no clear idea of his future. His sociable and open nature led him into financially perilous activities. He was to squander his inheritance.

Isabella Shawe
(above right) The couple met in London in 1835, married, and for four years were blissfully happy. Thackeray sketched her many times.

CHARTER 79 HOUSE. Gainsborough 1748.

Key Dates

1811 born in Calcutta

1815 father dies

1816 sent to England for his education

1817 mother remarries

1829 goes up to Cambridge

1830 leaves without taking his degree

1836 marries Isabella Shawe

1840 onset of Isabella's insanity

1845 Isabella committed to permanent care. Begins *Vanity Fair*

1855 lectures on *The Four Georges*

1857 loses Oxford by-election

1860 edits *Cornhill* magazine

1863 dies on Christmas eve

His gentleman's education continued at Trinity College, Cambridge, which he entered in 1829. Initially, he had high hopes of academic success, but instead of leaving with a degree, he took away with him two lifelong passions – for banqueting and for the theatre. He also acquired a dangerous taste for gambling. One evening, he was set up by a group of professional card-sharps, to whom he lost £1,500 – a sum he was not even due to inherit until he came of age in 1832.

COMING OF AGE

Thackeray abandoned his university career in June 1830, and within a month, he was preparing for a prolonged visit to Germany – in particular to Weimar, the country's cultural capital. For six months, he attended balls and dinners, flirted, met Goethe, and in mid-winter, hired sedan chairs to carry him through the snow to court. He was becoming a rake.

Back in England in 1831, Thackeray began training for the law. He applied himself for some months, but within a year he had given up his studies – informing his mother that 'this lawyers preparatory education is certainly one of the most cold-blooded prejudiced pieces of invention that ever a man was slave to'. He kept on his chambers in the Middle Temple as a *pied à terre*, and squandered his time and money lounging about London, drinking, fencing, womanizing and gambling at cards and dice. He was becoming a compulsive gambler, and his diary shows him to have been full of self-reproach at his idleness, and desperate to free himself from his urge to gamble.

In July 1832, Thackeray came of age, and celebrated with a trip to France, visiting galleries and theatres, reading French literature, frequenting the best restaurants – and gambling. In November, he returned to London and resolved to settle down and behave like a model young gentleman. He tried 'bill discounting' (a kind of money lending) for a short while, and then became involved in the less shady enterprise of buying and editing an arts-oriented newspaper, *The National Standard*. The paper lasted only a year, but by the end of that time, Thackeray had made his entry into London's literary scene.

Yet at this time he was more inclined to think of himself as an artist than as a writer. In 1833, he was painting in Paris – able to indulge his drawing ability, with no fear of having to make a living from it. But at the end of that year, his fortune – some of which he had already gambled away – disappeared almost completely with the collapse of the India banks in which his inheritance was invested.

Apparently undeterred, Thackeray continued his art studies – in London, and then in Paris. Lack of money seemed to free him rather than oppress him, and he enjoyed the Bohemian lifestyle of a Parisian artist: 'I was as poor as Job: and sketched away most abominably, but pretty contented: and we used to meet in each others little rooms and talk about Art and smoke pipes and drink bad brandy and water.'

It was not among the Parisian Bohemians, but among the English middle-classes in Paris that he met the young woman who was to become his wife. Isabella Shawe was small, shy, red-haired, naïve – and poor. They fell in love in 1835, and despite parental discouragement, married the following year.

At first they were blissfully happy, living in a tiny Parisian apartment, enjoying their new domestic routine. Thackeray was earning eight guineas a week for writing one or two articles for the *Constitutional and Public Ledger*, a paper which his step-father had bought. In 1837, the young couple returned to London, where their three daughters were born: Anne (born in 1837); Jane (born in 1838 but died in 1839), and Harriet (born in 1840). Thackeray was enchanted by his children, and deeply attached to his wife. In 1838, he wrote that they had 'been nearly 2 years married and not a single unhappy day'. He had no idea that their happiness was soon to be shattered.

Fine Art Photographic Library

Three months after Harriet's birth, he set off alone for Belgium's art galleries, against Isabella's wishes. She had been depressed since before her confinement and was now probably suffering from post-natal depression. Thackeray, on the other hand, thrived. He had 'a delightful trip, pleasure and sunshine the whole way'. But when he returned he was so alarmed by Isabella's mental state that he took her to visit her mother and sister in Ireland.

The journey was 'three days and four nights of hell', during which Isabella plunged into 'absolute insanity'.

Cambridge days
(above) Thackeray entered Trinity College, Cambridge half-way through the academic year, and left after only two years — with mixed feelings; 'three years industrious waste of time might obtain for me mediocre honors which I did not value a straw'.

○ *Fact or Fiction* ○

THE HAZARDS OF GAMBLING

Most of the gambling casinos of Europe were squalid places with an atmosphere of hysteria that concealed the financial tragedies enacted there. Thackeray himself gambled away his own inheritance, and used his experiences in *Vanity Fair*. Ironically, he found it a relief; 'My golden time was when I had no gold'.

Gambling hysteria
The English were reputed to be cold-blooded enough to stick to a system, but many privileged young men lost their fortunes.

Rowlandson: The Hazard Room. Victoria & Albert Museum/Bridgeman Art Library

Musée Carnavalet, Paris/Lauros-Giraudon/Bridgeman Art Library

Private Collection

Letters *to his daughters reveal his devotion.*

Minny and Anny
(left) While he pursued his career in London, Thackeray was forced to leave his growing daughters in care, and near their disturbed mother, in Paris. Later, they were to give his life its only real focus of affection. Despite the many obstacles, he was an ideal and devoted father who succeeded in making them feel secure through, as Anny observed, 'certainty of love far beyond our deserts'. Both daughters were to nurse him through his many illnesses.

A Parisian artist
(below) Reminding his mother that 'At twenty . . . we all thought I was a genius at drawing', Thackeray settled in Paris with his grandmother and 'made believe to be a painter'. Studying and copying old masters in the Louvre, 'It was a very jolly time'.

She attempted suicide by leaping into the sea where for 20 minutes she floated before being located. She had to be continually watched at her mother's, and was never left in sole charge of the children. At nights, Thackeray tied a ribbon linking their waists lest she made any further suicide attempts.

Thackeray was under enormous pressure, not least from his mother-in-law whom he had always disliked (whenever he wrote about an unhappy marriage there was always a pestering mother-in-law in the background doing her worst). Just as she was instruct-

ing him to put Isabella into an asylum, he took the family and fled to the safety of Paris.

His own mother took care of the children from 1840–45 at her home in Paris, while he divided his time between lodgings in London and Paris. From here Thackeray took Isabella round European clinics, vainly seeking a cure. In 1845 he gave up. He brought Isabella back to England and consigned her to the care of a Mrs Bakewell. The pressure began to tell; he visited her less and less until, at last he concluded, 'I think it best not to see her'. Nevertheless, her welfare remained of prime importance to him. Insane, Isabella was to outlive him by 30 years.

COMING TO TERMS

Thackeray had been forced to earn his living since he was 22. He worked as a freelance journalist during the early years of his marriage, writing reviews, comic sketches and art criticism for a variety of publications including *The Times* and *Punch*. Writing under pseudonyms, he used the name Michael Angelo Titmarsh (Michelangelo also had a broken nose); it was not until he was 32 that he wrote under his own name.

In 1845, the same year that he settled Isabella's future, Thackeray began *Vanity Fair* – his first major novel. It was published in 20 monthly parts in 1847-8, and was an instant critical success. But the Victorian reading public did not like its cynical attitude to society. And although *Vanity Fair* made Thackeray's literary reputation, it did not make him a vast amount of money. He received £60 for each instalment and £2,000 from the sales of bound editions, which was more than he had ever earned before, but by no means a fortune. Importantly, though, it did mean that as a great novelist, he could now command higher rates than he had previously received.

As a literary celebrity, Thackeray was much in demand by high society. He wrote that he spent his time reeling 'from dinner party to dinner party – I wallow in turtle and swim in claret and Shampang'. But apart from being a larger-than-life public figure, Thackeray was also a devoted and conscientious father to his daughters. At home in Young Street, Kensington, he

provided Anny and Minny with 'the best learning of all, love and usefulness . . . and the faith of home, its peaceful rest and helpful strength'.

This initial period of literary fame was also dominated by unrequited love. In 1842, Thackeray's friend from university days, William Brookfield, had introduced him to his wife, Jane. Thackeray's allegiance gradually swayed from husband to wife. It was a relationship in which Thackeray demanded more than Jane was ever prepared to give. She flirted with and confided in him, particularly when she had marriage problems, but they were never lovers. The end came in 1851 when her husband demanded that she finish with Thackeray.

It was in that year that Thackeray hit upon a new way of making money. He undertook a lecture series entitled *The English Humorists of the Eighteenth Century*. The readings in Willis's Rooms, St James's in London

were given on six successive Thursdays at three in the afternoon. They were so successful that the streets outside were packed with the carriages of aristocrats and writers. His enthusiastic audiences would have been shocked to discover that the self-conscious Thackeray thought his lectures worthless 'humbug' and 'quackery'. Nonetheless, they were both profitable and good experience for future lecture tours.

He lectured in America in 1852. The audiences, often numbering 1,200 a night, were as impressed by his appearance – he was six foot, three inches tall, approximately 16 stone, and had a huge head with a fine mop of silvery hair – as by his lectures. Returning home in 1853, aged 42, he was uncertain whether to continue lecturing or writing. He settled for writing *The Newcomes* and set off for Europe with his daughters, to gather source material. On their return to London in 1854 they moved into 36 Onslow Square, Kensington.

Thackeray's life was becoming increasingly punctuated by punishing bouts of illness. They were aggravated by a urethral problem – probably the result of a venereal disease contracted in his youth – and his excessive eating and drinking. While his body was slowly dying on him, his imagination – which he thought had also had its day and become an 'unexploded squib' – suddenly burst back into life.

Outraged by the suffering and injustice of the Crimean war, he lectured on *The Four Georges* in 1855,

Alfred, Lord Tennyson
(above) Thackeray enjoyed the admiration of the greatest writers of his day. Of Pendennis, *Tennyson said, 'It was quite delicious . . . a produce of the Man's Wit & Experience of the World'. He befriended the family.*

Jane Brookfield
(above left) Condemned, in his own words, to a life as a 'grass widower', Thackeray sought comfort from the wife of an old university friend. Her own unhappy marriage led her to welcome his circumspect advances.

Palace Green, Kensington
(right) 'it is one of the nicest houses I have ever seen', enthused Thackeray when buying his last house. The spacious rooms of the 'Palazzo', as the family called it, enchanted him.

saving his finest invective for an attack on George IV and the aristocracy. He was so scathing that London society more or less outlawed him for the next 18 months. Having discharged his radical fury, Thackeray returned to the profitable life of giving lecture tours and sailed for America.

The success of *The Four Georges* and of his standing as a lecturer prompted Thackeray to try for Parliament. He declined to stand at Edinburgh because his liberal views, advocating Sunday entertainment, would have been political suicide in Scotland, but he did fight the

Oxford by-election in 1857. However, the grand literary celebrity found the rough and tumble of street electioneering quite different from lecturing and lost, albeit by 1,005 votes to 1,070.

Thackeray was continually ill at this time. He retched so violently that he was often left 'half dead'. However, illness did not prevent him from editing and writing for the *Cornhill Magazine*, and enjoying the company of his two daughters. And since he was now financially secure, he lent money to his many friends.

In 1862 the Thackerays moved to 2 Palace Green, in Kensington. It became one of London's showpieces with its antique paintings, Corinthian pillars, marble hall and vast fireplaces. He set about a new novel, *Denis Duval*, and visited Rye and Winchelsea in Sussex for background information.

On 21 December, 1863, he dined with Charles Dickens, announcing that he had now completed the first four instalments of his novel. On Tuesday, he attended a funeral at Kensal Green, returning home 'very gentle and sad and cold'. On Wednesday he was ill again – his daughter Anny said that he just 'lay very still with large eyes . . . and said it can't be helped darling'. The following morning, just after she had got up, she heard a 'strange crying sound'. She found him 'lying back with his arms over his head, as if he tried to take one more breath'. He was buried at Kensal Green near his baby daughter Jane who had been brought there 25 years before. Two thousand people attended.

Portrait of an old man
(left) The recurring illnesses of old age kept Thackeray 'squeamish & ill' and confined to his rooms, intensifying the 'deep, steady melancholy of his nature'.

THE WRITER AS ARTIST

Thackeray's early promise lay not in writing but in drawing and painting. In the summer of 1833, he resolved to set up in Paris as an artist. Having left Cambridge without a degree, he felt obliged to assure his mother that in Paris an artist was 'by far a more distinguished personage than a lawyer & a great deal more so than a clergyman'. She was easily persuaded – 'we all thought I was a genius at drawing' – and he had already sold some caricatures.

For three years he studied and copied old masters, generally having a 'jolly time' but growing increasingly disappointed with his 'mean little efforts'. Marriage, and the attendant financial responsibilities, finally ended his artistic aspirations – in 1836 he took a job as Paris correspondent with the *Constitutional and Public Ledger*. Yet art remained an interest throughout his life. He often illustrated his letters, and continued to take pleasure in sketching his family.

A facility for comic drawing
Despite advice from George Cruikshank (Dickens' illustrator), Thackeray could not rise above caricature.

VANITY FAIR

In his famous novel of people "making love and jilting . . . cheating, fighting, dancing and fiddling", Thackeray creates riotous comedy out of human folly and weakness.

The great English conductor, Sir Thomas Beecham, rated *Vanity Fair* as the greatest novel of the Victorian period, perhaps because of those qualities that characterized Beecham's own conducting: wit, flair and sparkle. It is an indictment of stupidity, greed and hypocrisy that sizzles as it stings. The satire is so uproarious, and written with such style that it was applauded by the very society it was aimed at.

GUIDE TO THE PLOT

At its simplest level, *Vanity Fair* is the tale of two heroines, Becky Sharp and Amelia Sedley, who have just graduated from Miss Pinkerton's academy, – a finishing school for young ladies – and who are heading in the same coach for the big wide world. The innocent, gently-reared Amelia has been immaculately 'finished' for her entry into society. The rebellious, low-born Becky is all set to make her way in it by her wits.

Before taking up an appointment as governess in the household of Sir Pitt Crawley, Becky stays in the Sedley home. There she makes an immediate play for Amelia's physically and financially ample brother, Jos. He, though enchanted, is manoeuvred away from making a proposal by George Osborne, Amelia's snobbish fiancé, who does not want to marry into a family with 'low' connections.

Becky is thus compelled to take up her employment at the Crawleys. The Crawley household includes the comically mean

baronet Sir Pitt, his neglected wife, and his sons Pitt and Rawdon. Over this motley family Becky soon reigns supreme, and even captivates Rawdon's rich aunt and benefactress.

After the death of his wife, Sir Pitt proposes to Becky, who is now forced to confess that she is already married – to his son, Rawdon. Sir Pitt is driven "insane with baffled desire", and Rawdon is cut out of his aunt's will.

Becky's social difficulties and marital problems are paralleled, in a more sombre key, by Amelia's. Her impending marriage to George Osborne is threatened when her family sinks into financial ruin and George's father

An opening flourish
(left) Becky Sharp's defiant spirit makes itself felt immediately. On leaving school, she is presented with a "Dixonary" – and wastes no time in flinging it straight back. Full of unladylike spleen, she is more than ready to take on the 'real' world.

Vauxhall frolics
(below) An evening at Vauxhall gardens ends Becky's first 'campaign'. She is within inches of a proposal from the "big beau" Jos Sedley, when he orders the famous Vauxhall "rack punch" and proceeds to get gloriously drunk – to the delight of all but his companions.

Henry Nelson O'Neil: Before Waterloo. Fine Art Photographic Library

Mary Evans Picture Library

Before Waterloo
(above) The order to march is given, and soldiers bid a hasty farewell to wives and sweethearts – not least among whom are Becky and Amelia. Becky of course is as composed as "the great Duke himself", while an inconsolable Amelia looks on as George prepares to leave. He is thrilled that at last "the great game of war was going to be played and he one of the players". But glory – and George – are shortlived.

Brighton reunion
(below) Dobbin joins the "principal personages" at Brighton, and brings them news of Napoleon's advance on Belgium.

refuses to countenance a union between his son and a "lame duck's daughter". However, inspired by his friend William Dobbin, who is himself in love with Amelia and always selflessly thinking of her happiness, George rebels against his father and marries her.

George is killed at the battle of Waterloo, and Amelia is so poverty-stricken that she is

J.C. Maggs: The Arrival of the Royal Mail, Brighton. Fine Art Photographic Library

> "'... while that little pink-faced chit Amelia, with not half my sense, has ten thousand pounds and an establishment secure, poor Rebecca (and my figure is far better than hers) has only herself and her own wits to trust to.'"

The betrothed
(below) 'Intended' for each other since childhood, George and Amelia seem secure in their courtship – until Amelia's family faces financial ruin.

Charles Spencelayh: Cupid Serenading Lovers. Fine Art Photographic Library

forced to entrust the welfare of her beloved son, Georgy, to her despised father-in-law. Dobbins remains devoted to her, but Amelia is blindly attached to George's memory.

Meanwhile, Becky is skilfully managing a difficult entrance into high society "on nothing a year". However, she tends to overplay her hand. Her husband Rawdon is apprehended for his debts and Becky seems reluctant to bail him out of the spunging-house (where debtors were held before prison). When Rawdon is freed, thanks to the generous intervention of his sister-in-law, he arrives home to find his wife in a compromising situation with the sinister Lord Steyne. Abruptly, their marriage is over and Becky must again fend for herself.

As Becky's fortunes decline, so Amelia's rise, for old Mr Osborne dies, leaving a substantial inheritance for his grandson and restoring guardianship of the boy to Amelia. Becky leaves for the Continent, where she is shunned by polite English society, but, nothing daunted, tries to enlarge her small annuity by gambling. In the final part of the novel, Becky confronts Amelia and Jos Sedly once again, and it is Becky who is instrumental in radically altering the lives of her old London friends.

Vanity Fair is a profound social satire, the society in question being that of early 19th-century England. The values of this society are based on money and class – twin sources of power. What fascinates Thackeray is the struggle for social supremacy between an out-moded aristocracy, clinging to its status and privileges, and the newly-rich middle classes anxious to buy themselves into high society.

THE DISEASE OF SNOBBERY

Vanity Fair shows snobbery from both sides. It is about people who feel superior to others simply because of their social background. As a boy at public school, Dobbin suffers grievously because of this attitude. He is ridiculed and victimized by his school fellows for no other reason than that he is the son of a grocer, rather than a son of a 'gentleman'.

But *Vanity Fair* is also about people who bow and scrape to those of higher rank, and seek to emulate them. This trait is most savagely portrayed in the person of old Mr Osborne, who, "whenever he met a great man

A widow's solace
(left) Prostrate with grief after George's death, Amelia is only saved by the birth of her son, Georgy. On him she lavishes all her care and tenderness, and he – like his father – repays her with patronizing good humour. The two live in acute poverty, and Amelia's maternal feelings are torn between love for her son and the desire to do the best for him – by giving him up to the rich Osborne relations.

he grovelled before him, and my-lorded him, as only a free-born Briton can do." Nearly all the cruelty, treachery, vanity and hypocrisy in the novel comes from this disease of snobbery, which itself arises from the hilarious but unseemly scramble for money and social position.

The ironies and illusions behind this scramble are underlined by Thackeray when he catches certain characters alone, suddenly confronting the hollowness of their lives. Old Mr Osborne, having parted wrathfully from his son George over his 'low' marriage, later – after George's death – feels a shuddering

> "… a title and a coach and four are toys more precious than happiness in Vanity Fair…"

terror "as if he had been the author of the doom which he had called down on his son." Even Becky is not immune. Her life without Rawdon is lonely and wretched, despite her resourcefulness. "She was, in fact, no better than a vagabond upon this earth. When she got her money, she gambled; when she had gambled it, she was put to shifts to live . . ."

Yet, for all the incisiveness of his criticism, Thackeray never loses his buoyancy. The novel teems with life and detail, and the very energy of his satire counteracts the pessimism of his outlook. Thackeray certainly shows us that "Vanity Fair is a very vain, wicked, foolish place, full of all sorts of humbugs and falsenesses and pretensions", but he does so with a delicious sense of humour.

In the Background

PRESENTATION AT COURT

A court debut was polite society's ultimate seal of approval. Thus "many a lady whose reputation would be doubtful otherwise and liable to give infection, passes through the wholesome ordeal of the Royal presence, and issues from it free from all taint." Thackeray's heroine, Becky Sharp, typifies the low-born social climber, eager for respectability. After her encounter with the King, the "French rope-dancer's daughter" takes to a virtuous life in comical earnest, cutting all the ladies of dubious reputation she has previously known, because "'One must, my dear, show one is somebody . . .'"

A glittering array
(below) Lace, brocade and diamonds reflect the degree of importance attached to a court occasion – and allow the wearers, like Becky, to play the part of an empress, if they choose.

Social acclaim
(left) After Waterloo, Becky channels her considerable charm, talent and energy into securing a place in London society. She courts the socially great and powerful, especially the old cynic Lord Steyne. But her popularity with such men jeopardizes her reputation, so that even as "she was writhing and pushing onward towards what they call 'a position in society' . . . the servants were pointing at her as lost and ruined."

humbug, that low-bred cockney, that padded booby". In so doing she gets belated revenge for George's sabotaging of her relationship with Jos. As she herself says, "Revenge may be wicked but it's natural."

It is Becky's malicious sparkle and her resilience which make her attractive despite her total lack of principle. She is intrepid where Amelia is insipid, and the pure-bred English rose pales in comparison with the worldly-wise, green-eyed artist's daughter.

Crucially, however, Thackeray makes very clear the reasons for Becky's unscrupulous actions – namely, the "dismal precocity of poverty", which in a world governed by money, privilege and pedigree has spurred her to fight for those very goals herself. Amelia is equally the product of her class and upbringing, and her goal of husband-getting forms the fabric of her life, even though the idea is swathed in romance and orange blossom – "those touching emblems of female purity imported by us from France, where people's daughters are universally sold in marriage". A suitable (wealthy) husband for Amelia is no less important to her than it is to Becky, but it is Amelia's parents who concern themselves with "suitability", while she is free to daydream about her chosen lover. Along with Thackeray we cannot help lamenting that "poor Emmy had not a well-regulated mind".

One of his gifts is for combining humour and pathos, as in the character of Jos Sedley. Jos's vanity, his dandyism and bashfulness, make him a riotously funny character, but also an intrinsically sad one. He lives like a 'gay young blade', but in reality "were it not for his doctor, and the society of his blue-pill, and his liver complaint, he must have died of loneliness."

Thackeray makes two women the pivot of the novel, and through them examines two differing visions of womanhood, the one ideal, the other seriously flawed. Amelia is passive, loving and loyal in true Victorian

style. Becky is the opposite – treacherous, greedy and dangerously dynamic. Where Amelia is a doting mother, Becky is a cold and selfish one.

Yet Thackeray makes his two main characters more complex than a simple contrast between good and evil would allow. Becky's disloyalty to the admirable Rawdon may be reprehensible, but Amelia's unthinking fidelity to the memory of the unworthy George is equally wrong. Becky, unlike Amelia, is intelligent and sees people for what they are. We are glad that she finally punctures Amelia's illusions about George – "that selfish

"A NOVEL WITHOUT A HERO"
This subtitle to *Vanity Fair* acquires many meanings as the novel progresses. It refers to the two heroines with their respective capacity to twist men around their little finger (Amelia thus exploits the incorruptible Dobbin, and Becky exploits every man but Dobbin, for all other men are eminently corruptible)

Vanity Fair questions the whole notion of the hero, and so implicitly criticizes Amelia for hero-worshipping George. Thackeray cuts him down to size in a chillingly brutal description of his inglorious death:
"Darkness came down on the field and city; and Amelia was praying for George, who was lying on his face, dead, with a bullet through his heart."

The startling realism of this passage is Thackeray's weapon for attacking the false heroism of contemporary novels. Part of the fun and fascination of *Vanity Fair* lies in its deliberate reversals of the conventions in which the morally censorious Victorian age gloried. Thus, the ideal woman is shown up in all her inadequacies, and neither marriage nor death provides a comfortable solution to life's problems. Thackeray refuses to explain or justify dubious actions or circumstances, nor does he believe in poetic justice. He pays his readers the compliment of being able to make their own judgments, and wants them above all to question rather than to accept.

Rawdon is 'wanted'
(right) Becky's debut in society is financed by a finely orchestrated series of debts. She keeps the creditors at bay in a variety of ingenious ways – until one night Rawdon is taken away to be an unwilling guest at the bailiff's "dismal place of hospitality". Becky prevaricates about bailing him out, and the episode triggers a drastic change in their lives.

Thackeray builds his characters through a combination of description and dialogue, but there are two other facets of his art that bring his characters to life: his authorial comments and his illustrations. As a novelist, Thackeray makes his presence felt by his observations, be they satirical, droll, straightforward or ambiguous. And his illustrations for *Vanity Fair* reveal his vivid and often hilarious conception of these 'puppets'.

WHO'S WHO

Rebecca (Becky) Sharp   The daughter of a penniless artist and a French dancer. She uses her wits to promote herself in society, with no regard to principles. As she herself says " 'I'm no angel' ".

Amelia Sedley   The prize product of Miss Pinkerton's academy for young ladies – "a dear little creature", she is sensitive, demure and good – and destined to become a 'model' wife.

William Dobbin   A grocer's son. Socially clumsy and self-effacing, his personal and military courage make him the novel's closest approximation to a hero.

Rawdon Crawley   Becky's husband and chief conquest – "a very large young dandy". His bluff, inarticulate nature conceals a lonely, courageous spirit – and a proud heart.

George Osborne   Amelia's sweetheart, and Dobbin's fellow-officer. His snobbishness and pomposity are fostered by his City-rich father. He dies "for Glory" at Waterloo.

Jos Sedley   Amelia's brother, the "collector of Bogley Wollah". Timid, self-indulgent but magnificently affected, he is a true figure of fun.

Miss Crawley   Rawdon's overfed and worldly aunt, courted by all her relations for her money.

Sir Pitt Crawley   Becky's first employer and subsequent suitor – "a more cunning, mean, selfish, foolish, disreputable old man" does not exist in the whole baronetage of England.

W.M. Ray: Girl at the Opera. Fine Art Photographic Library

Victoria & Albert Museum/Bridgeman Art Library

Jos Sedley (above) flees both romantic and military campaigns when they become too dangerous. He escapes Becky and Waterloo, but is to meet the former again…

"Dobbin of ours" (left), lisping, gauche and shy, is a shining example of strength and honesty – yet even he is flawed by his adoration of the 'unworthy' Amelia.

A.E. Chalon: Girl Reading a Letter. Fine Art Photographic Library

"Our gentle Amelia" (above) is a dutiful daughter, a selfless mother but an ambiguous heroine. Her wilful attachment to George's memory leads her to abuse Dobbin's genuine feelings for her, and earns her the novelist's final stinging epithet of "tender little parasite".

George Osborne (right) "famous in field-sports, famous at a song, famous on parade" is popular with men and patronizing to women. Vain and superficial, his undoubted physical courage is seen as a substitute for moral strength.

The "little adventuress" **Becky Sharp** (above) has sparkling green eyes, wit, charm and a superb acting ability. Her treacherous nature is offset by an admirable toughness and good humour, and wherever she goes in society she has "all the men on her side", while she fights the women "with indomitable courage". Dazzled by her brilliance, Rawdon believes in her "as much as the French soldiers in Napoleon".

Miss Crawley (right) has "a balance at her banker's which would have made her beloved anywhere", and which is particularly attractive to her Crawley relations and to Becky. A free-thinking, reprobate old lady, she despises yet plays upon her sycophants, and adores Becky's malicious and irreverent humour.

Fine Art Photographic Library

ROLLICKING SATIRE

Spurred on by ambitions to retrieve his fortune and die wealthy, Thackeray worked at a furious pace, wrily lampooning the breed of people he knew best.

'Papa, why don't you write books like *Nicholas Nickleby*?' Thackeray's younger daughter, Minny, once asked him. Many of Thackeray's contemporaries thought of him and Dickens as competitors, although Thackeray himself insisted that they were quite different. He greatly admired Dickens' exuberant, larger-than-life characterizations, but his own aim was to stay close to real life.

Thackeray's sense of history was particularly strong, and he was sensitive to the changes that had overtaken English society and made it 'Victorian'. Yet, unlike Dickens, he paid relatively little attention to specific social abuses that might be put right by human action. Books such as *Vanity Fair, Henry Esmond* and *The Newcomes* imply that society lives by false values that distort and override what is good in human feeling. For his characters, as for himself, life is essentially a struggle between virtue and wrong-doing.

It was his need for money, after he lost his fortune in the India bank collapse, that drove him to write, and for years he worked in relative obscurity as a journalist, struggling for survival rather than literary fame.

But his productivity was remarkable, especially once he had a wife and family to support. Reviews, essays, travel impressions, and stories – comic, burlesque and satirical – flowed from his pen. Michael Angelo Titmarsh, George Fitz-Boodle Esquire, and other Thackeray pseudonyms appeared regularly in the pages of *Fraser's Magazine* and *Punch*. In the years before he began *Vanity Fair*, he published *The Yellowplush Papers, The Great Hoggarty Diamond, The Book of Snobs, Barry Lyndon* and many other works, for the most part sparkling and high-spirited. At this stage in his career, Thackeray found that deadlines actually concentrated his mind: 'I love to hear the press thumping, clattering and banging in my ear; it creates the necessity which always makes me work best.'

AT HOME AND ABROAD

Being restless and sociable, Thackeray also found it hard to work in one place for very long. Much of his writing was done 'on the run', during holiday jaunts such as a trip to Belgium, which consisted of 'having good dinners and sleeping on benches of afternoons and writing between times'. He clearly enjoyed the atmosphere of hotels, clubs, and pubs like Don Saltero's in Chelsea, where he wrote up his trip *From Cornhill to Grand Cairo*.

This taste was reinforced by his domestic circumstances. Working at home with a wife and children in the house proved difficult. And for a time, when his wife had gone mad, Thackeray was forced to compose with his children shut up in one room and Isabella 'raving' in another. Even after Isabella was taken into care, and he was involved in his substantial major novels, Thackeray complained that London was impossible as a workplace, whereas Paris was 'like perpetual Champagne'.

Writing full-length novels was a far more sustained and laborious task than his journalistic pieces had been, and Thackeray found the required effort no easier as the years passed. He procrastinated as much as he dared, despite

'Earthy we are and of the earth' wrote Thackeray when attacked for passing no moral judgements on his characters. He found both good and bad (to varying degrees) in himself and everyone around him. He was a participating member of 'salon society' (right) and had succumbed in his youth to many of its vices. However, though he does not adopt tones of high moral censure, it would be a mistake to find no moral standpoint in his books. His satire is a subtle, oblique form of criticism which, once glimpsed, has a delicious humour.

Writer on the move
William never set his writing to one side. Wherever he went he mustered material and inspiration, and committed them to paper. He was a great traveller, too, as his various travelogues witness. This ornate and compact travelling desk (right) went with him on every trip.

Private Collection

Garrick Club/E.T. Archive

Mary Evans Picture Library

Young journalist
At 22 Thackeray (left) took the helm of the National Standard *(right). The journal floundered, but William was launched on a literary career. He ended life as editor of the successful* Cornhill Magazine *(far right).*

London Library

British Library

A meeting in Rome
When researching The Newcomes *William went to Rome, combining business with a holiday The character of the hero grew out of a meeting he had there with the artist Lord Frederick Leighton.*

Panini: The Coliseum. Fine Art Photographic Library

his fixed principle of writing at least a line every day. 'When I am in labour with a book I sit for hours before my paper, not doing my book, but incapable of doing anything else and thinking upon that subject always, eating with it, walking about with it, and going to bed with it.'

His letters are full of complaints about the drudgery of writing, his failures of inspiration, his feeling of being creatively exhausted. In the last decade of his life he found some relief in dictating the narrative, most often to his daughter Anny. Yet Thackeray's emotional involvement with his characters was intense. When he reached the scene in *The Newcomes* in which Colonel Newcome dies, he stopped dictating, sent Anny away, and went on, pen in hand, by himself. And at the end of each novel he experienced heart-rending pangs at parting with his shadow-people whom he had come to think of as old friends: 'That finis at the end of a book is a solemn word.'

Some of Thackeray's difficulties arose because he could not afford to wait for inspiration, since he was writing for money. He signed contracts to deliver unwritten novels in monthly parts, whether or not he had any idea of what they were to contain. Serialized publication was a strain for Thackeray, who did not work to a preconceived plan, but improvized as he went along – with the result that he often had to send to the printer for the earlier sections to safeguard against inconsistencies or repetitions.

Consciously, at least, Thackeray wanted money for the sake of 'my three little girls' – his two daughters and his hopelessly insane wife. His fears for their future were reasonable enough, since he had seen a number of his apparently vigorous male friends die prematurely, leaving wives and children destitute and dependent on the charity of friends. However, although Thackeray saved steadily to reach his target of £20,000 (the fortune he should have inherited from his own father), he also spent lavishly when his writing began to command high prices, perhaps to make certain the target was never reached.

Working for money appears to have been at least partly a psychological device. It kept him tied to his desk, and it allowed him to feel that he would have been able to produce novels of much higher quality if he had not needed to drive up his income. It is just as likely that a financially secure Thackeray would have stopped writing altogether.

Money-making, however, also distracted and exhausted him. One of Thackeray's most profitable but least taxing ventures was lectur-

Familiar faces
William's mother was his inspiration for 'Helen Pendennis', his stepfather for 'Colonel Newcombe'.

Private Collection

ing. In 1851 he shrewdly launched the first series, *English Humourists of the Eighteenth Century*, at the height of the fashionable season, amid the gilding and blue damask of Willis's Assembly Rooms at St James's. 'Duchesses were there by the score', wrote Charlotte Brontë, who also attended. The lecture was a triumph, and Thackeray went on to tour England, Scotland and the United States, in spite of his literary commitments and what he called his 'hawful state of health'.

It is possible, however, that his money-drive marred as well as made him. In 1859, when he was earning the huge sum of about £5,000 per year, he could not resist taking on the editorship of the new *Cornhill* magazine for another £1,000. In combination with novel-writing, the extra work may well have brought on Thackeray's fatal illness.

But Thackeray did not always work simply for the money. His lectures on *The Four Georges* were inspired by his anger at the horrors of the Crimean War. He satirized all four monarchs unforgettably, but his portrait of George IV is the most savage. An overfed

dandy who spent millions, he is perceived as nothing more than the sum of his clothes. Thackeray opposed "the right divine of kings to govern wrong".

Thackeray was, however, a man of contradictions, and was very much at home in that 'old society of wits and men of the world' which his lectures centred on. This affinity led him to set several of his novels including *The History of Henry Esmond* and *The Virginians*, in the 18th century.

Henry Esmond, published five years after *Vanity Fair*, was a new departure for Thackeray not only in being set in the previous century, but in being planned and written in its entirety before publication. It appeared in 1852, at a time when the historical novel was out of fashion, but it was hailed as a masterpiece. Thackeray himself hoped that he would 'stand or fall by Esmond'.

But despite the ease with which he adopts 18th-century style and idiom, Thackeray's concern for the truth cuts through historical convention. In the first chapter, for example, he wastes no time in deflating the "French

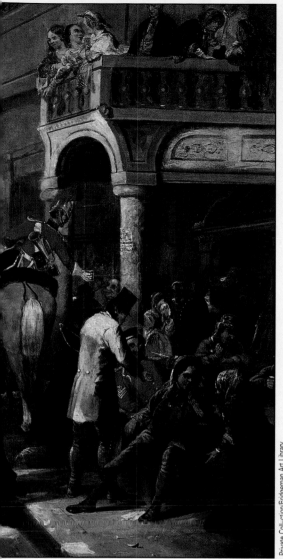

Private Collection/Bridgeman Art Library

Set in the past
(right) Many of Thackeray's works were period pieces, set in the 18th century – an era with a special appeal for him. The human foibles he portrayed were, of course, timeless.

Outraged by war
(left) Nursing severe doubts, as a young man, about the merits of monarchy, William learned to suppress his opinions rather than antagonize the royalists among his readers. However, the pointlessness of the Crimean War and its ultimate squalid horror so shook him that he was stirred to write the most savage of attacks against the King he held responsible. As a result, he was shunned for more than a year.

Gainsborough: The Duke and Duchess of Cumberland and Lady Elizabeth Luttrell. Reproduced by gracious permission of Her Majesty the Queen

King Lewis the Fourteenth", who, *"divested of poetry . . . was but a little wrinkled old man, pock-marked, and with a great periwig and red heels to make him look tall."*

STRENGTH OF CHARACTER
Beatrix, with whom the hero is in love, is vain, beautiful and ruthless in her ambition to marry a powerful, wealthy husband. In pursuit of her aims, Beatrix has sacrificed both the ability and the need to love, a fact she admits with chilling candour. She confesses to Esmond that when she heard that her betrothed had died, " 'I was frightened to find I was glad of his death; and were I joined to you, I should have the same sense of servitude, the same longing to escape'. "

This kind of human paradox, where a wrong course is pursued in preference to a right one is typical Thackeray. Throughout his work he shows his understanding of the complex origins of human action, base or perverse as they may be. And one of his gifts is his ability to express such insights with extraordinary simplicity. For him, human na-

ture is unchanging and what is true for a fairy tale should also be true for a complex novel. His fairy tale *The Rose and the Ring* has just this kind of pure psychological truth.
So the Lady of Honour and the Prime Minister hated Giglio because they had done him a wrong.

And in *The Newcomes*, for example:
The father and son loved each other so, that each was afraid of the other.

Thackeray is unusual among his contemporaries in being a commentator rather than a moralizer. He presents the truth as he sees it, and leaves the reader to ponder the moral issues involved. His aims and his practice are summed up in the Preface to *The History of Pendennis*: 'I ask you to believe that this person writing strives to tell the truth. If there is not that, there is nothing.'

American triumph
'. . . though I don't love America I love Americans with all my heart.'
Thackeray's two lecture tours were hugely successful – especially the vitriolic attacks of the Four Georges. Pictured left is the 1852 New York lecture on English Humorists.

Thackeray was never a hack, but often considered that he sacrificed excellence to profit. By the end of his life, his unkindest critics agreed.

Barry Lyndon (1844) was a promise of things to come, though some misinterpreted its moral stance. *Vanity Fair* (1847) achieved matchless acclaim, though a perfection of the Thackeray style came later. The serialized *Pendennis* followed (1848-50), its strengths lying in characterization, not plot. *Henry Esmond* (1852) was not serialized, and Thackeray hoped to 'stand or fall' by it and, indeed, many call it his finest work.

The return to serial form was constricting: interest was never allowed to flag. But criticism of the sequel to *Pendennis, The Newcomes* (1853-55) is that it drags. *The Virginians* (1857-59) was equally disappointing.

The author's opinion of his work is hard to deduce, since he was ready to heap scorn on his every effort.

THE LUCK OF BARRY LYNDON
◆ 1844 ◆

Redmond Barry (above) degenerates from likeable rogue to card-sharp before marrying and persecuting the wealthy Countess of Lyndon. On the surface, this is the self-glorifying autobiography of an adventurer. But Barry's complacent account 'unintentionally' reveals his vicious self-seeking. Only when the Countess's son reaches manhood does Barry's luck run out. Remarkable for its unsparing, unsentimental treatment of human failings, the book was mistakenly taken at face value by many and was not a success.

THE HISTORY OF PENDENNIS
◆ 1848-50 ◆

Love for an actress (left) is the first act of folly committed by Arthur 'Pen' Pendennis, the reckless son of Helen, a loving but over-indulgent mother. Prevented from making a disastrous match by his worldly wise uncle, Major Pendennis, Pen wastes his time at university and gets into debt, but is saved by Helen's adopted daughter, Laura Bell. She helps him to make a literary career in London where he shares chambers with the upright George Warrington – another good influence. But, this time encouraged by the Major, Pen becomes involved with the wealthy, accomplished but shallow Blanche Amory. His relations with a working-class girl, Fanny Bolton, further complicate matters, outraging both Helen and Laura (though Pen has in fact resisted the temptation to take advantage of Fanny). Only after many complications does Pen reach maturity and win his true love. Dicken's *David Copperfield* appeared at the same time as *Pendennis*, and the two novels, both markedly autobiographical, are often compared.

THE HISTORY OF HENRY ESMOND ESQUIRE
◆ 1852 ◆

Marlborough's wars against the French (below) feature in this, Thackeray's finest historical novel. Henry, supposedly illegitimate, discovers he is the true Lord Castlewood, but honourably conceals the fact out of devotion to the incumbent Lady Castlewood. Out of love for the cold, worldly Beatrix, he plans a coup to restore the Pretender: Beatrix's silly flirtation defeats it. Disgusted with English politics and society, Esmond turns to the woman who has always loved him.

Victoria & Albert Museum

THE NEWCOMES
◆ 1853–55 ◆

Clive Newcome (above) loves his cousin Ethel, but scheming relatives want her to make a grander alliance, and Clive is persuaded to marry a woman with whom he has nothing in common. Clive's father, Colonel Thomas, is a man of real goodness, but his obsessive love for his son brings them both unhappiness. Intent on bequeathing a large fortune, he ruins himself by speculation. Clive's wife and the Colonel die. Meanwhile, despite the pressures on her, Ethel has refused to marry. A happy ending is implied.

THE VIRGINIANS
◆ 1857–59 ◆

Scenes of colonial and Anglo-American warfare (right), and a narrative split between two heroes made *The Virginians* more episodic and less successful than the other major novels. Set in America a generation later than *Henry Esmond*, it chronicles the fortunes of Esmond's twin grandsons, George and Henry Warrington. The serious-minded George is believed killed fighting the French. Happy-go-lucky Henry finds himself heir to his mother's Virginian estates. As such, he is taken up by his corrupt Castlewood relations when he visits England: one of them, Baroness Bernstein, is Esmond's old love Beatrix, now a cynical old woman. Under their influence, Henry lives wildly, falls into debt, but is rescued by George – not dead at all, but simply held prisoner by the French. Both George and Henry marry against the wishes of their domineering mother, and she disowns them. The bond between brothers remains unbroken, even though they take opposite sides during the War of Independence. Ultimately, each finds the society and country that suits him best.

Library of Congress/BPCC/Aldus Archive

The Shadow of Napoleon

The French Revolution unleashed energies and passions that swept all Europe into war. One figure rose above the tumult to personify the threat, the power and the nameless fears.

The year Thackeray was born, 1811, saw Britain and much of the Continent of Europe engaged in a desperate war with the armies of Revolutionary France – a war that had already raged for 16 years and was to continue for a further six. Although as an infant Thackeray lived in India, remote from war, it fascinated him in later years, and was to play a central role in his masterpiece *Vanity Fair*. In the novel, the great events of the closing years of the wars with Napoleon, from the Battle of Leipzig to Wellington's triumph at Waterloo, are linked with the personal histories of Becky Sharp and Amelia Sedley.

On the whole, the English gentry and bourgeoisie were remarkably untroubled by the war – although a few, like old Mr Sedley in *Vanity Fair,* were financially ruined (or made) by the turn of events, and young aristocrats in their dashing uniforms would set young ladies' hearts aflutter thinking of the dangers their paramours might face. Yet it was a war both Britain and France, the two main protagonists, threw themselves into with great ferocity. Unusual for modern warfare, neither side would settle for less than total victory. It was to be, the British Prime Minister William Pitt informed the House of Commons early in the war, 'a war of extermination'.

'OLD BONEY'

At the centre of the conflict was the figure – small in stature but vast in power and influence – of Napoleon Bonaparte. Napoleon was, some have argued, 'the most powerful genius who ever lived'. A brilliant soldier, his remarkable military victories made many believe he was utterly invincible, as Joe Sedley echoes fearfully on the eve of Waterloo in *Vanity Fair*: "Napoleon! What warrior was there, however famous and skilful, that could fight at odds with him?"

In the minds of many English men and women, though, Napoleon was an evil, ruthless tyrant. To old Mr Sedley, ruined by Napoleon's 'comeback', he was the 'Corsican scoundrel from Elba', while a generation of English nursemaids terrorized naughty children with dire threats of 'Old Boney'. When Thackeray was six, the ship bearing him from India to England stopped at the lonely island of St Helena where Napoleon was

David: Napoleon Crossing the Alps, Charlottenburg Castle Berlin/Fabbri/Bridgeman Art Library

Napoleon Bonaparte
(right) In this magnificent painting, the French painter Jacques-Louis David portrayed Napoleon heroically as the great war leader – a warrior fit to rank with Charlemagne.

Josephine Beauharnais
(left) Soon after he first became famous in 1796, Napoleon married Josephine, the widow of a French aristocrat executed by the Revolution. She bore him two daughters and became his Empress in 1804. But when she failed to give him a son, he annulled their marriage and married the daughter of the Austrian Emperor.

Napoleon at bay
(right) The allies' view of Napoleon, 'the Corsican ogre' was considerably less than heroic – especially after his defeat at Liepzig.

The Battle of the Pyramids
(above) In 1798, Napoleon's expeditionary force swept through Egypt and into Syria. But the defeat of the French fleet at the Battle of the Nile ended the campaign.

in exile after the war. After a long trek across the island, Thackeray's servant pointed out a man walking and whispered to the young boy: 'That is he, that is Bonaparte! He eats three sheep every day, and all the little children he can lay hands on!'

Like his military tactics, Napoleon's career was marked by breathtaking speed. In 1791, at the age of 22, he was a lieutenant in the Revolutionary Army. A year later, he was captain. A year after that he was a national hero. That year, 1793, as Louis XVI went to the guillotine and the Revolution turned increasingly bloody, France was torn by internal rebellion even as she threw down the gauntlet to the world. It was Napoleon who engineered an artillery siege that ensured the capture of the rebellious port of Toulon for the Revolutionary Army.

Further successes elevated him to the command of the French Army of Italy in 1796. In a lightning cam-

paign across northern Italy, he scored a dozen resounding victories in as many months and brought Austria to its knees with an army of less than 30,000 men.

Given command of the French Army of England, he set about planning the downfall of France's greatest enemy. After careful study, Napoleon concluded that a direct assault across the English Channel would fail, so he chose an audacious attack – through Egypt to India, which would devastate Britain's economy.

The French expeditionary force which set sail in May 1798 met with initial success: first Malta, then Alexandria and the Nile delta falling before it. But a crushing defeat at the hands of Horatio Nelson in the Battle of the Nile on 1 August ruined Napoleon's grand design, stranded the army and left him to escape back to France alone.

The failure in Egypt did nothing to diminish his ambitions, nor to harm his prospects. Within a month, he had conspired in a successful *coup d'état* and emerged as First Consul. He went on to become First Consul for Life in 1802 and finally crown himself Emperor in 1804. But from the moment of the *coup d'état* in November 1799, he was effectively master of France.

25

Baron de Steuben: Napoleon. Fine Art Photographic Library

Revolutionary hero
Though his enemies feared and despised him, there is little doubt that his soldiers – and the risen but leaderless masses of post-Revolutionary France – revered him. His part in the popular uprising that had swept France – to the accompaniment of the guillotine – and his dazzling military successes gave a focus to the enormous energies that had been released. Even Thackeray felt compelled to speak in the Cambridge Union on the subject of 'Napoleon as a Captain, a Lawgiver, and a King merited & received the esteem & gratitude & affection of the French Nation'.

There was only the briefest of pauses while Napoleon consolidated his power. Then, in spring 1800, he struck at the Austrians again, in northern Italy. After struggling through the snow-covered St Bernard Pass, the French fell upon the Austrians and defeated them at Marengo on 14 June. With the Austrians out of the war, Britain and France glared at each other in hatred across the Channel, but it was stalemate – thunder as they might against 'Boney', the British could not challenge him on the Continent, while Napoleon could not bring down 'this nation of shop-keepers' with the British fleet still controlling the seas. In mutual frustration, the two nations signed a peace treaty at Amiens on 25 March 1802.

The peace of Amiens could not last; it was no more than an armed truce between two irreconcilable enemies. A year later, the war resumed, and resumed in such a way as to give the British a real fright. With no-one left on the Continent who dared to fight him, Napoleon concentrated his entire military might on a cross-channel invasion. Over the next two years, a Grand Army was assembled at the Channel ports, and some 2,000 flat-bottomed boats were built to transport 10,000 soldiers across to England.

But to invade England, the French had to control the English Channel. Napoleon's strategy was to lure the British fleet into the Atlantic, so that a combined French and Spanish fleet could sweep unopposed up the Channel to rendezvous with the invasion flotilla. What happened, in fact, was that the French fleet under Admiral Villeneuve was hounded back and forth by Nelson and finally driven to take refuge in Cadiz. On 19 October 1805 Villeneuve ventured forth to do battle – against his better judgement, but on the express orders of an incensed Napoleon. Two days later, his

fleet was annihilated off Cape Trafalgar, and the great invasion scare was lifted.

On the Continent the war raged on. Crushing victories over the Austrians at Ülm, and over combined Austrian and Russian forces at Austerlitz on 2 December 1805, made it plain that on land France was still invincible. Prussia entered the fray belatedly in 1806, only to have her armies destroyed at Jena and Auerstadt. And if there was still any doubt as to who was master of Europe, it was settled in the summer of 1807, at Friedland, where the Grand Army inflicted 25,000 casualties on the Russians.

Trafalgar had destroyed Napoleon's hopes of invading Britain, but he might still beat her by wrecking her trade – by totally excluding her from Europe. To do this, he first had to seal off Britain's entry to the west. And so it was that Napoleon turned his gaze on the Iberian peninsular and Portugal, Britain's old ally.

THE PENINSULAR WAR
Within a year, the French had occupied Lisbon; within two, Napoleon's brother Joseph was on the throne of Spain. But then Napoleon encountered a new problem: the Spanish and Portuguese people rose up against the French. The years of savage guerilla warfare that ensued allowed the British to establish a bridgehead on the Continent and made the name of Sir Arthur Wellesley, later the Duke of Wellington, as Commander of the British army in the Peninsular.

Britain's other entry to the Continent was via Russia, where the Tsar, despite the earlier Treaty of Tilsit, turned a blind eye to his merchants' evasion of the trade ban. But if Napoleon's attempt to subjugate Spain and Portugal was a mistake, his move against Russia was a disaster.

Retreat from Moscow
(below) The turning point in Napoleon's career was the terrible retreat from Moscow in 1812, when the Grand Army was decimated by their struggle home in bitter cold and without food.

R.C. Woodville: Retreat from Moscow. Fine Art Photographic Library

In Spring 1812, Napoleon amassed a force of half a million men and struck out for Moscow. Seventy five miles short of the goal, on 7 September 1812, one of the goriest engagements of the war was fought to a standstill – the Battle of Borodino. Technically a French victory, since the Russians withdrew leaving Moscow deserted and blazing, it cost Napoleon as dear as any defeat. He held Moscow, it was true, but the Russian capital was a ruin, the Russian army had not come to terms, and worst of all, they had left behind a land ravaged and bereft of food. Napoleon had no alternative but to retreat before the onslaught of the Russian winter. So began one of the most ghastly episodes in the history of war. Starving, freezing, stumbling through blinding snowstorms, harassed on all sides by Russian snipers and decimated by the icy torrents of the river Beresina, the tattered remnants of the Grand Army straggled back to Poland. Of the 600,000 who entered Russia, barely 100,000 returned.

The retreat from Moscow shattered the myth of Napoleon's invincibility, and soon Britain and her allies were closing on his battered army. At the Battle of Leipzig, in October 1813, the Grand Army was smashed; in November, Wellington crossed the Pyrenees; in December, the Prussians crossed the Rhine. Twist and turn as Napoleon might, in a dazzling series of defensive manoeuvres, there was no escape. On 31 March 1814, the victorious allies entered Paris, Napo-

leon was sent into exile on the isle of Elba, and the powers of Europe sat down in Vienna to divide up the spoils of war.

The Congress of Vienna was still sitting ten months later when the news came 'like a bombshell' that Bonaparte had escaped from Elba: "In the month of March, Anno Domini 1815, Napoleon landed at Cannes, Louis XVIII fled, and all Europe was in alarm, and the funds fell, and old John Sedley was ruined." For 100 days, the Napoleonic legend lived again, as the former Emperor gathered an army of peasants and soldiers large enough to "disturb the peace of Europe".

The myth shattered
(above) The disastrous flight from Russia 'snuffed out' the myth that Napoleon was invincible on land and opened the way for a renewed allied assault on his decimated army, an assault that was to drive him to exile in Elba.

The Duchess's Ball
(above right) On the eve of Waterloo, while Napoleon's army was launching its first attack on the allies, barely 20 miles away in Brussels, the English were fighting for tickets to the Duchess of Richmond's glittering ball and, in Vanity Fair, Becky was flirting with George. In the early hours of the morning, many soldiers left the ball for the battle.

News from Waterloo
(left) When they read of the victory at Waterloo in the Gazette, 'all England thrilled with triumph and fear'. Only later came 'the sickening dismay when the lists of the regimental losses were gone through', naming the dead. Thackeray himself visited the famous battlefield years later – it was a sight that moved him deeply: 'A man of peace has no right to be dazzled by that red-coat glory, and to intoxicate his vanity with . . . carnage and triumph'.

Wellington boot
(below) The Duke of Wellington was hailed as England's saviour after the victory at Waterloo, and became a hero to many. He also gave his name to a new style of footwear, modelled on his riding boots.

Immediately, the British and Prussians began to re-mobilize, while Napoleon went on to the offensive, marching his Old Guard into Belgium to confront the armies marshalling against him. Few expected him to move quite so fast and, in Brussels, the British Army, along with the George Osbornes, the Rawdon Crawleys and all of Vanity Fair, were having a ball. "There never was . . . such a brilliant train of camp-followers as hung around the Duke of Wellington's army in the Low Countries in 1815; and led it dancing and feasting, as it were, up to the brink of battle."

On 15 June, while English society revelled at the Duchess of Richmond's ball in Brussels, Napoleon advanced within 25 miles of the city and had already engaged an English troop. The next day, the Prussian army under Blücher was sent scurrying from Ligny while Wellington clung desperately to Quatre Bras. On the 18th, the final confrontation took place at Waterloo, not far from Brussels.

WATERLOO FIELD

"All day long, whilst the women were playing ten miles away, the lines of the dauntless English infantry were receiving and repelling the furious charges of the French horsemen." Then just as all seemed lost, the English were reinforced by the Prussians, and Napoleon's Guard turned and fled.

30 years after the battle, William Thackeray visited Waterloo before starting work on *Vanity Fair*. 'Let an Englishman go and see that field,' he wrote in *Fraser's Magazine*, 'and he *never forgets it*.' Yet Thackeray felt it was wrong to wallow in false glory, condemning it as 'egotistical, savage, unchristian'. 'A man of peace has no right to be dazzled by that red-coat glory, and to intoxicate his vanity with those remembrances of carnage and triumph . . .'

As for Napoleon, he was taken under armed guard aboard *HMS Bellerophon* to the remote isle of St Helena, where the infant Thackeray saw him little more than a year later. Bonaparte died in 1821, a sad embittered man, maintaining to the end that 'If the English had let me, I would have lived in peace.'

ANTHONY TROLLOPE

1815-1882

H. O'Neil: Anthony Trollope/1873. The Garrick Club, London/E.T. Archive

Convinced, with good reason, that he was unloved and unregarded,
Anthony Trollope struggled long and hard for a foothold in the
world. But his vast resources of energy and dogged hard work broke
down the barriers to success and found him loved, fêted and avidly
read. His labours were Herculean. He pitted himself against Time to
produce a library of books about credible people and their credible
foibles. His readers responded by recognizing Trollope as a shrewd,
honest, wry portrayer of English life.

'A Good Roaring Fellow'

Disregarded and undervalued, Trollope suffered a childhood of neglect and poverty. By sheer hard work, he achieved personal happiness and literary success, earning the accolade 'a Trojan of a man'.

The life of Anthony Trollope might have been written by a novelist, or conceived by a writer of fairy tales. Neglected and unloved by his parents, he survived a childhood of unrelieved misery. At school he suffered almost every form of injustice which small boys are capable of perpetrating against one another. In his youth and early manhood he felt himself to be a failure, his life not worth living. Then suddenly and dramatically, his fortunes changed. In a few short years he found wealth, a wife, happiness and a creative energy almost unique in the history of literature.

Anthony Trollope was born in Keppel Street, Bloomsbury, London, on 24 April 1815, the fourth child in a family of six. Thomas, the eldest, was born in 1810 and was his mother's favourite. Only he and Anthony survived past maturity.

Their father, Thomas Trollope, was a conscientious and serious barrister, but with an extraordinarily difficult temperament. His hectoring, arrogant manner proved a severe handicap to his career – so much so that his practice failed totally. Rather in the manner of Dickens' character Pip, he had 'great expectations'. In this, as in almost everything, he was to be disappointed. The inheritance he believed to be his slipped through his fingers when his childless benefactor remarried unexpectedly at the age of 60 and fathered six children. The disappointment deepened a constitutional gloom such that

it was said of him by his eldest son that he induced a state of acute anxiety in all those who were thrust into his company.

After a series of unsuccessful attempts to revive the family fortunes, Thomas Trollope retreated into a solitary and unreal world, writing a monumental encyclopedia of all known ecclesiastical terms. When he died at the age of 61 he had just reached the letter 'D'.

A FORMIDABLE MOTHER

Anthony's mother, Mrs Frances Trollope, was another formidable personality. She was devoted to her husband, energetic, pretty, strong-willed and hopelessly extravagant. Unable to live within her means, it was her recklessness with money, as much as her husband's ineptitude, that caused their financial ruin. And although she was devoted to Tom, her eldest son, to Anthony she showed an indifference bordering on negligence.

With such parents it is scarcely surprising that Trollope's early years were disturbed. Tired of his failing career, Mr Trollope rented a tract of farm land near Harrow on which he built a large house, 'Julians'. From here all three Trollope boys (Tom, Henry and Anthony) were sent to Harrow, the fashionable public (private) school. As non-boarders they paid no fees, and were looked down upon by the other boys. To make matters worse, they were badly clothed, with

National Portrait Gallery, London

Frances Trollope
(left) This resourceful mother was forced to draw on every ounce of her remarkable stamina. But for Anthony she had little maternal feeling, and later did not even read his books.

Harrow School
Here Trollope suffered "a daily purgatory". An atmosphere of barbaric violence prevailed (right) and he was despised as a day-boy. A contemporary recalled, 'He gave no sign of promise whatsoever . . . and was regarded by masters and boys as an incorrigible dunce.'

Harrow Local Collection

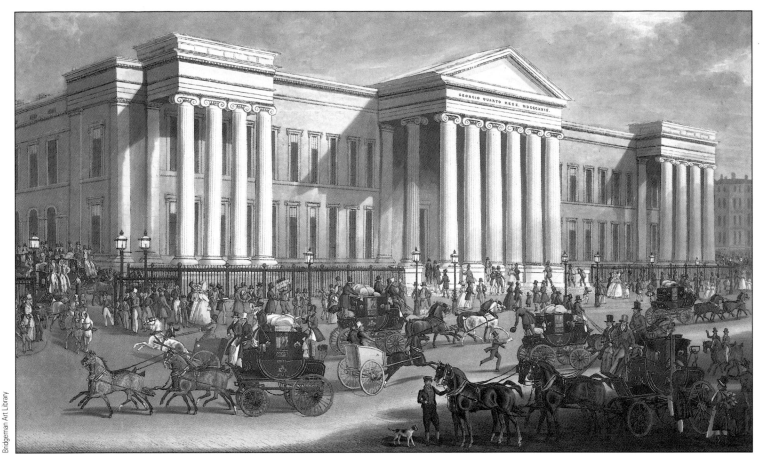

Bridgeman Art Library

The Post Office
Trollope escaped the horrors of schooling when he was given a clerk's job at St Martin's-le-Grand in London (above), the administrative heart of the Post Office.

shoes always down at heel. Even in old age neither Tom nor Anthony was able to forget or forgive their father for having sent them there.

When he was 10, Trollope was sent on to Winchester, his father's old school. He fared better there, but not much. His elder brother was a prefect at the school and his mother had urged him to watch over Anthony. This he did with a vengeance. Anthony was to write years later in his *Autobiography*, 'in those school-days he [Tom] was, of all my foes, the worst . . . Hang a little boy for stealing apples, he used to say, and other little boys will not steal apples . . . The result was that, as part of his daily exercise, he thrashed me . . .'

OVERSEAS FOLLIES

Anthony was still at Winchester when his mother conceived the idea of opening an emporium in Cincinnati in the United States. She travelled there, and her husband and her children followed – except Anthony. He was left behind to fend for himself. From the age of 12 to 15, he never saw his mother. After two years the Trollopes returned to England, having lost what little money they had. But the time had been considerably worse for Anthony.

While the family was away, Anthony's school fees were not paid; local tradesmen ceased to give him credit and his allowance was stopped. He had no home to go to during the school holidays, and spent one summer vacation wandering about the deserted law buildings of Lincoln's Inn, his father's old chambers. Suicide seemed a possible escape: 'how well I remember all the agonies of my young heart; how I considered whether I should always be alone; whether I could not find my way to the top of that college tower, and from thence put an end to everything?'

Clerical drudgery
(right) Office work did not suit his temperament. He found it very hard to "live in London, keep up my character as a gentleman, and be happy" on £90 a year. With his family abroad, he eked out a seedy, listless existence in lodgings. At this low point, he wrote nothing, convinced of his worthlessness.

Mary Evans Picture Library

On the family's return, Anthony was removed from Winchester, penniless and in disgrace, and sent once more to the much-hated Harrow. From 'home', a small, derelict farmhouse, he walked to school every day in battered boots and mud-stained clothes. 'Poor Trollope was tabooed', recalled a classmate. 'He gave no sign of promise whatever . . . I avoided him for he was rude and uncouth.'

Back at home in England, Frances Trollope wrote *Domestic Manners of the Americans,* and on the strength of its great success, 'Julian's Hill', a larger, more comfortable house, was acquired. But within two years, the accumulated debts of a lifetime caught up with the Trollopes. Fearing imprisonment in the Marshalsea – the debtors' prison in London known intimately to Dickens' parents – the family escaped to Bruges in Belgium before the bailiffs arrived. Anthony remained in England, alone.

Oxford would have been open to Trollope had his schooling not been bungled. Instead, when he was 19, his mother obtained a commission in the Austrian cavalry for him, and also used her influence to arrange an interview for him at the General Post Office in St Martin's-le-Grand, London. Anthony chose the Post Office position although his education had done very little to equip him for any career. Asked to produce a sample of his handwriting, Trollope managed only a smudged, blotted scrawl. Totally ignorant of even simple arithmetic, he was relieved when told that he would not be tested until the following day, and even more relieved when on returning the next day he was informed that the test had been waived.

GOING TO WASTE

After ten years of schooling, Trollope had acquired only a shaky grasp of Latin and Greek; no other subject had been included in the curriculum. At 19, however, he joined the Post Office. He was to remain in its service for the next 33 years.

Little was expected of him, although even that he found difficult. Being polite and obsequious – the only qualities demanded of a very junior clerk – did not come naturally to him. The work was dull and repetitive, and he loathed it. Alone in London, living in miserable lodgings off the Marylebone Road, he felt his life wasting away.

Outside office hours he went for long walks (some-

times covering as much as 30 miles a day), got drunk on gin, and read. But it was no life for someone of his energies and talents. At 24, feeling his life to be not worth living, he suffered an illness which nearly killed him. What the illness was, no-one knew, but it was probably connected with his state of mind at the time. Apart from the circumstances of his daily life, he had much to be depressed about. His brother Henry had died a lingering, painful death from consumption in Bruges, and his father had fallen ill and died shortly afterwards. Negligent as ever, so far as Anthony was concerned, his mother did not think of summoning him to either his father's or his brother's funeral.

At 26 it seemed that Anthony Trollope was destined to follow in his father's footsteps — to be a disappointed and frustrated man. But then a vacancy for a Post Office Surveyor's clerk occurred in the south of Ireland, and to his astonishment he was given the job.

Ireland was to be the making of Trollope. As luck would have it, he was asked to carry out many of the duties of the Surveyor, whose job it was to travel the region on horseback inspecting post offices, investigate complaints and chart new postal routes. Trollope loved almost every aspect of the work: the open air, the people he encountered and the handsome salary he was paid. It was here too that he was introduced to hunting – a passion that was to remain with him for the rest of his life.

In Ireland, all Trollope's longings and latent powers

Forbes Magazine Collection, New York/Bridgeman Art Library

A HOUSEHOLD NAME

The daughter of an eccentric country parson, Frances 'Fanny' Trollope was an unusually free-thinking woman for her time. She emigrated to America with her children (except Anthony) to join an idealistic community. She found conditions there "vividly dreadful", but was determined to open a general store in Cincinnati. It failed. Returning to England aged 52, she wrote, in sheer desperation, a first book: *Domestic Manners of the Americans*. The Americans hated her for it, and years later, when Anthony visited the States, they were still smarting at her insults. But it was a best-seller in Britain and was followed by 40 more books. Her novels annoyed the Establishment, for they made outspoken attacks on child labour and the New Poor Law. In later years she lived in Florence with her eldest son, Tom, at the Villino Trollope.

Wealth at last
Fanny (right) produced roughly two books a year, the last appearing when she was 76 and living in luxury in Florence.

Robert Harding Picture Library/Boston Public Library

'The Factory Boy'
(left) Social injustice was a favourite target for Fanny's writing. She wrote vigorous, hard-hitting books with plenty of violence and pathos. Most were illustrated by her companion in Cincinnati, Auguste Hervieu.

Mansell Collection

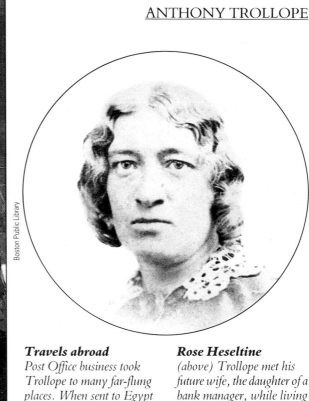

Boston Public Library

Travels abroad
Post Office business took Trollope to many far-flung places. When sent to Egypt (left) he took the opportunity of making a private excursion to the Holy City, Jerusalem.

Rose Heseltine
(above) Trollope met his future wife, the daughter of a bank manager, while living in Ireland. Their marriage produced two children and lasted the rest of Trollope's life.

Trollope always claimed that before September 1843 he had never put pen to paper. By the time of his marriage, however, he was more than half-way through his first novel, *The Macdermots of Ballycloran*. His mother arranged for its publication, but did not bother to read his work.

A NEW DEPARTURE

If literary success was not instant, Trollope's career at the Post Office prospered. In 1851, he was given the job of reorganizing the postal service in south-west England, and in 1854 was promoted to Surveyor. It was while visiting Salisbury that the idea of 'Barchester' was first formed. With the publication of the first of the Barchester novels *The Warden*, in 1855, his name began to be noted in the literary world. And with *Barchester Towers* (1857) he became more widely known to the reading public.

In old age, Trollope claimed that from his youth his life had been unusually happy, although there is little evidence to support this. He did have a rare talent for enjoying himself, but his ceaseless activity and obsession with work may have fulfilled a psychological need. It was as if he feared idleness, or that too much time on his hands would plunge him into feelings of insecurity or depression.

Appointed Chief Surveyor in charge of the eastern counties, he moved, in 1859, to Waltham House in Waltham Cross, Hertfordshire. Here he enjoyed the best years of his life. His daily timetable was gruelling in the extreme, yet he thrived on it. It began at 5am with a cup of coffee. At 5.30 he was at his desk reading and revising the previous day's work. At 9.30 he stopped writing, having completed 2500 words. After a substantial breakfast, he took the train to London,

National Gallery of Ireland

Riding to hounds
(above) While in Ireland, Trollope took up hunting, and came to "love it with an affection which I cannot myself fathom". Despite his being heavy, short-sighted and often short of funds, "Nothing has ever been allowed to stand in the way of hunting".

were realized. He was a changed man. In place of the shy, retiring, nervous youth, unsure of himself and of his place in the world, a big, blustering man appeared, exuding energy and self-confidence. He began to enjoy life to the full.

Within months of his arrival, he met his future wife. Little is known of Rose Heseltine, the daughter of a Rotherham bank manager. Several years his junior, she was small, attractive, shrewd and witty. Whether they continued to be happy or contented together is not known, but their marriage lasted from 1844 to Trollope's death. They had two sons, Henry, born in 1846 and Frederick, in 1847.

The Writer's Life

Mansell Collection

Love and approbation
Trollope craved affection and, in mid-life (left), won it in plenty. One friend called him 'a good roaring fellow', another 'crusty, quarrelsome, wrong-headed, prejudiced, obstinate, kind-hearted and thoroughly honest'. "The Garrick Club [right] was the first assembly of men at which I felt myself popular," wrote Trollope (standing fourth from left). His illustrator, John Everett Millais, leans on his cue, far right.

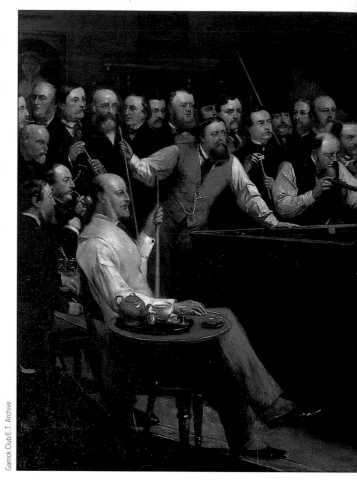

Garrick Club/E.T. Archive

A valued friend
(below) Trollope met Kate Field while visiting Italy. Young, talented, free-thinking and ambitious, she captivated all the distinguished men she met, including the now-famous novelist.

arriving at his office at 11.30. Working to 5.00pm he then retired to the Garrick Club for tea and a rubber of whist, returning home for dinner at 8.00pm.

Trollope entertained lavishly, and enjoyed eating and drinking. When a guest once remarked that he seemed to enjoy a healthy appetite, he replied in typically bluff manner, 'Not at all, madam, but, thank God I am very greedy.'

Two days a week he forgot the cares of the Post Office, and hunted in the company he enjoyed best – farmers and country gentlemen. He also found time to travel extensively, combining official business with pleasure. Often accompanied by his wife, he would go armed with a commission to write a travel book. He visited Egypt, the West Indies, America (twice), Australia (twice, staying with his son Frederick, a sheep farmer) and South Africa. In addition, he was a regular visitor to his mother and brother Tom at the family villa (Villino Trollope) in Florence, where in 1860 he met Kate Field, a young, rich and cultured American.

A CHOSEN FRIEND

In his *Autobiography*, he described her as 'one of the chief pleasures . . . of my later years.' To him she was 'my most chosen friend . . . a ray of light'. At the time of their meeting Kate was 21, he 45. Their relationship was almost certainly platonic. But they wrote to each other frequently. They met seldom – when he visited America, or she London or together at the 'Villino Trollope' in Florence. He assumed the role of teacher and advisor to her. She never married, but continued to intrigue and court the attention of famous men, and women, throughout her life.

In his career, things went well but not to the extent he might have wished. Promotion to the highest level at the Post Office eluded Trollope, and he never made as much money from his books as Dickens and Wilkie Collins had. But he seemed satisfied with his lot, as

Boston Public Library

Royal Commonwealth Society/E.T. Archive

Visit to Australia
(above) Anthony's son Fred emigrated to Australia to run a sheep farm. He was notably unsuccessful, and lost his father a lot of money. Two visits by Anthony and Rose, however, were cheerful excursions and gave rise to a travel book and two novels, the best of which was John Caldigate.

34

Parliament [should be] the highest . . . ambition of every educated Englishman'). He lost badly, coming bottom of the poll.

Having retired early, Trollope forfeited his pension. He sold Waltham House and moved to Montague Square in London. From here he continued to write, to attend his clubs – the Garrick and Athenaeum – for tea, whist and conversation. But as his health deteriorated, he was advised to move to the country. He took a renovated farm-house. 'Harting Grange', near the Hampshire/Sussex border. But away from his beloved clubs and the noise and bustle of London, he became bored. With few visitors and little to do, he aged rapidly. He continued writing, but in his heart felt that life was slipping away.

NO MORE WORDS

His wife arranged for him to stay for a while at Garlands Hotel in the West End of London, hoping that back in the city his spirits would revive. He visited his clubs again and dined out, but at Alexander Macmillan's, the publisher's, he suddenly fell off his chair, one evening, paralyzed down his right side. Rushed to hospital, he lingered there for a month, unable to speak a word – dying on 6 December 1882. For a man who gloried in language, it was a painfully silent death.

A tribute in the magazine *Vanity Fair* during his life paid him a grudging compliment which Trollope may have prized above any other: 'His manners are a little rough, as is his voice, but he is nevertheless extremely popular among his personal friends'. All his life, Trollope had wanted just that.

novels continued to pour from his pen at a remarkably regular rate. He rode with the hunt well into his 60s, and loved the activity "with an affection which I cannot myself fathom".

In 1867 Trollope resigned from the Post Office. Resentment at having been passed over in promotion may have been part of the reason, but a more practical one was the offer of the editorship of the *St Paul's Magazine*. It proved to be a false step. Trollope lacked the necessary qualities to make a good editor, and the magazine failed. He then stood as a Liberal candidate for Parliament ('I have always thought that to sit in . . .

Fact or Fiction

THE REAL BARCHESTER

In 1852 Trollope visited Salisbury and, "wandering there one midsummer evening . . . I conceived the story of *The Warden* . . . stood for an hour on the little bridge and . . . made out the spot on which Hiram's Hospital should stand". But in the book, he likens Barchester to "Wells or Salisbury, Exeter, Hereford or Gloucester". There is no real Barchester. It was invented by a man who "never lived in any cathedral city – except London".

Look-alikes

The Bishop of Clifton declared he knew Barchester to be Wells in reality, for it had two towers. Trollope retorted that it was not Wells at all, but Winchester (below).

Victoria & Albert/Bridgeman Art Library

BARCHESTER TOWERS

**This novel does not deal in thrills and adventure. Instead it assembles
a set of very familiar people and makes their small hopes and
anxieties matter as acutely as our own.**

A t the outset of *Barchester Towers*,
Anthony Trollope comments drily:
"There is perhaps no greater hardship
at present inflicted on mankind in civilised and
free countries than the necessity of listening to
sermons." It is an ironic comment from an
author who excelled at the portrayal of clergymen and who once likened the writing of
novels to the preaching of sermons. Yet there
is little of the soap-box in his book, and more
of the soap opera. Its continuing appeal has
less to do with Trollope's moral oratory than
his insight into character, his gift for comedy,
and his fascination with the intrigues that
underline the apparently placid surface of a
close-knit community.

GUIDE TO THE PLOT

The Bishop of Barchester has just died and, to
the disappointment of his son, Dr Grantly,
who had hoped to replace him, an outsider is
appointed as his successor. It soon becomes
plain that the new bishop, Dr Proudie, is a
weak man under the influence of his formidable wife and devious, self-serving chaplain,
Obadiah Slope. Slope quickly antagonizes
much of Barchester, particularly Dr Grantly
and Grantly's soft-spoken father-in-law, Septimus Harding. For Slope's sermons attack
the traditional, orthodox features of their
church services.

Originally a protégé of Mrs Proudie, Mr
Slope quarrels with the lady over who should

'The cursed sofa'

(right) Mrs Proudie is
determined to make her
mark on Barchester as
the new Bishop's wife.
She holds a lavish
party, but is outshone
by a far more glamorous
newcomer, the lame
Signora Madeline
Neroni. When the
Signora's brother
playfully pushes her
sofa and its castor rips
the train off Mrs
Proudie's dress, a cloud
gathers over Barchester
which will not disperse
nearly as readily as the
guests do from the good
lady's house-party.

Piety and tradition

(above) All Barchester
gathers eagerly to see
the new Bishop and to
hear his chaplain
preach. And what do
they hear? That their
practices (such as
singing and music) are
those of a "high-and-
dry church" and must
be swept away. The
Archdeacon declares
war, but good old
Septimus Harding, a
particularly fine
musician, sinks into
weary sadness and
needs the comfort of his
daughter (right).

36

be appointed warden at Hiram's Hospital, a charitable alms-house. Mrs Proudie wishes her husband to appoint Mr Quiverful, a rector with 14 children. Slope, however, begins to press the claims of Mr Harding, who recently resigned the post because of scurrilous criticisms of him in the Press. Needless to say, Slope's motives are far from pure. He wants

stiffness and formality . . . agreeable to Eleanor after the great dose of clerical arrogance which she had lately been constrained to take".

Unknown to Eleanor, Bertie's sister Charlotte is scheming on his behalf to secure their marriage. So too is his other sister, Madeline, until she perceives that Eleanor and Arabin are, without realizing it, in love.

"Bore of the age"
(right) Trollope has scant regard for the 'new' clergyman and takes time out from his story to make wry mock of ecclesiastical posers and their tricks of the trade. "The bible is good, the prayer-book is good, nay, you yourself would be acceptable, if you would read to me some portion of those time-honoured discourses … But you must excuse me, my insufficient young lecturer, if I yawn over your imperfect sentences, your repeated phrases, your false pathos, your drawlings and denouncing, your humming and hawing, your oh-ing and ah-ing, your black gloves and your white handkerchief." We are left in no doubt that Obadiah Slope is just such a clergyman.

Bridgeman Art Library

This kind of tactic is completely at odds with the elaborate mechanisms used by Wilkie Collins or Charles Dickens to maintain suspense. It struck Henry James as both a 'terrible crime' and 'a betrayal of a sacred office', since it drew attention to a novel's artifice. Yet this deliberate intrusion by Trollope is very revealing of his intentions and beliefs about the role of fiction.

For him, the plot of a novel, although a necessary device, was always the most insignificant part of a tale. He wished to maintain a comfortable relationship with his readers, and

> **"He is the most thoroughly bestial creature that ever I set my eyes upon," said the archdeacon.'**

to marry Harding's daughter, Eleanor, recently widowed and moderately wealthy. By arguing her father's case with the Bishop, he means to ingratiate himself with Eleanor.

Eleanor is also the subject of two other men's romantic aspirations. She attracts the attention of Bertie Stanhope, the charming, idle son of an absentee clergyman summoned home by the Bishop. A wealthy wife will release him from the necessity of working for a living. Eleanor's third suitor is the new vicar of neighbouring St Ewold's, the Reverend Arabin, who falls genuinely in love with her, but whose criticism offends her.

Arabin, Harding and Dr Grantly discuss her relationship with Slope in a way she finds most disagreeable, thus strengthening her resolve to be perfectly fair and friendly to the "bestial" chaplain. She is glad to get away from her over-protective family to the Stanhopes' where there is "an absence of

In the meantime, Harding and Dr Grantly are in despair at the thought of Slope marrying into the family. There is even a possibility now of Slope replacing the dying dean of Barchester. Trollope, as he weaves a just course for his characters, settles their fates, both clerical and romantic.

COMEDY AND INTRIGUE

The diverse elements which Trollope draws together so skilfully in *Barchester Towers* make it a perfect poise between clerical comedy and Victorian romance. Curiously, although the romantic intrigues in *Barchester Towers* are a potential source of suspense, Trollope reveals his plans for Eleanor at an early stage. At the end of Chapter 15 he declares his hand:
I would not for the value of this chapter have it believed that my Eleanor could bring herself to marry Mr Slope, or that she should be sacrificed to a Bertie Stanhope.

he was less interested in building suspense than in developing character. He rather enjoyed poking fun at the artificiality of contriving a plot:
How easily would Eleanor have forgiven and forgotten the archdeacon's suspicions had she but heard the whole truth from Mr Arabin. But then where would have been my novel?

What mattered to Trollope was the 'picture of common life enlivened by humour and sweetened by pathos'. It has been said that the great novelists offer one of two things to a reader – either surprise, or recognition. If so, Trollope offered recognition. He does not dazzle with narrative ingenuity; instead he delights in an authentic account of human nature.

Trollope neither idealizes nor condemns his characters. He depicts Mr Harding as a thoroughly good man (he is the true hero of the piece) but is not blind to the man's faults:

indecision, timorousness and gullibility. Dr Grantly is also an admirable man, but Trollope does not hesitate to convey his moral wrestling, at his father's death-bed, with the instinctive stirrings of ambition. Madeline Stanhope is a flirt and a coquette, but she stops short of causing lasting damage when she perceives that true love is at stake.

The humorist and the moralist in Trollope are perfectly illustrated in the scene where the odious Obadiah Slope proposes to Eleanor. Emboldened by champagne, he tries to embrace her, and receives a hearty slap across the face, which "resounded among the trees like a thunder-clap". It seems a fair retribution for his slimy courtship, his attempted seduction of Olivia Proudie, his fawning infatuation with Madeline Stanhope, and his machinations to secure the preferments he thinks he deserves. His shock is funny, but also salutary, for the just deserts of pride and ambition have been meted out.

STIRRED NOT SHAKEN

The major theme of *Barchester Towers*, treated first comically, then seriously, is the impact of change on tradition. The plot traces the effect on a conservative cathedral community of an

Mansell Collection

Rejected proposals
(left) One summer day brings an embarrassment of suitors to the feet of Eleanor Bold. She is unwilling to side with those who shun and malign Obadiah Slope, and her Christian charity gets her into difficulties behind the privet hedge – Slope, spurred on by her kindness and a passionate ardour for her money, makes his move. But Eleanor is quite able to look after herself (left). Bertie Stanhope, the good-natured waster, has been encouraged to propose by his sisters. He is easier to deter since his heart is not on the task.

Portrait of John Jenkins by Millais. Jesus College, Oxford

In the Background

THE GUTTER PRESS

Newspapers are seen as a corrupt, meddling, manipulative force in *Barchester Towers*. Slope uses them to further his political ambitions, and Harding remembers with dread, how their scandal-mongering ousted him from his previous job.

Trollope's attitude is made crystal clear. While he believes in the public's 'right to know', he is deeply suspicious of irresponsible journalism because it reduces complex issues to little more than inhumane, over-simplified and sensationalist absolutes.

'Talking points'
As the popular Press expanded in the 19th century, a new editorial element made its appearance: sales-boosting gossip. Fleet Street publisher Lord Northcliffe called these often sensational titbits 'talking points'. Answers magazine pandered to the new taste for trivia, with articles on 'What the Queen Eats' and 'How to Cure Freckles'. A cartoonist of the time lampoons gullibly avid readers, right.

Mansell Collection

exotic foreign influence (in the shape of Madeline Stanhope) and an ambitious, young, radical cleric.

Madeline, or the Signora Neroni as she chooses to call herself, somewhat disconcerted Victorian readers, yet proved to be one of Trollope's most unusual and intriguing inventions. Her lurid background (which includes marriage to a dissolute Italian, who may or may not have crippled her, and a child born shortly after her marriage) seems only to add to her allure. Unable to walk with ease, she "made up her mind, once and for ever, that she would never stand, and never attempt to move herself". But her beauty is such that not only Slope but Arabin and even Squire

Yale Center for British Art, Paul Mellon Collection

accepted

John Everett . 1853

known that the family of the Slopes will never starve;" he writes, "they always fall on their feet like cats, and let them fall where they will, they live on the fat of the land."

For all that the Signora and the chaplain disturb the peace of Barchester, they never seriously threaten it. But while it is true that Trollope was resistant to change and felt at ease with Victorian values, he saw plenty at fault with them. Tensions seethe beneath the calm civilities of his prose. He loves Mr Harding, and presents him as morally irreproachable, but the portrait is reflective and wistful, not energetic. Trollope loathes Slope, but he

> *"…you will not be insane enough to publish any of your doings in Barchester. Do not think I have not heard of your kneelings at that creature's feet – that is if she has any feet – and of your constant slobbering over her hand?… Clergymen have been unfrocked for less than what you have been guilty of."*

Arabin accepted
(left and above) A newcomer to Barchester, Arabin is installed as vicar of St Ewold, and is the Archdeacon's ally in the war against Slope. Arabin is a foil to the more foolish and villainous characters in the book. He is literate, moderate, thoughtful, articulate, honourable, and eventually wins the hand of the woman he loves.

Fine Art Photographic Library

Pawns in the game
The Quiverfuls of Puddingdale (left) and their 14 children feature in the power game between Slope and Mrs Proudie. The post of warden at Hiram's Hospital must go either to Quiverful or to Septimus Harding. Each contender has scruples about getting the better of the other, but to Slope and Mrs Proudie such competition is simply the stuff of politics.

Thorne fall under her spell. From her sitting position, she plays the role of enchantress, and the image Trollope uses of her is that of a spider "that made wondrous webs and could in no way live without catching flies."

KEY CHARACTERS
Madeline's function in the novel is a versatile one. She ruffles the complacency of a stolid community; she brings together Eleanor and Arabin; and she deflates – with hilarious effect – the pretensions of both Slope and Mrs Proudie. She also inspires some bizarre black comedy. When Mrs Proudie rounds on Slope for kneeling at the Signora's feet, she adds maliciously, "that is, if she has any feet."

Slope's impact on the community is equally marked. He is a 'new broom' who compels Barchester, however unwillingly, to re-examine some of its old values. As a Trollope creation he is quite extraordinary – from his religious beliefs to his lank red hair, there is nothing about him that the author likes. He is an authentic comic monster. Critics have felt Trollope went too far with Mr Slope, yet he is a timeless portrait of the ambitious opportunist who craves power and who is a guileful, ruthless operator in a world of naïvely honourable men.

Poetic justice demands that he should be defeated. But Trollope understands the ways of the world too well for that. "It is well

shows that, if Slope learns nothing, he loses nothing either – he is a survivor. Trollope does not let sentimentality blind him to some of the world's injustices.

Trollope survives in the esteem of readers partly for nostalgic reasons and partly for the sharpness of his observations. His writing reveals his understanding of individual foibles and the variety of human behaviour discernible in everyday life. This is what his fellow writers Hawthorne and Tolstoy found admirable. As an example of Trollope's inimitable talkativeness, humour, honesty and what Henry James called his 'complete appreciation of the usual', *Barchester Towers* could never be bettered.

CHARACTERS IN FOCUS

Trollope felt he owed a lot to his characters and was affectionately grateful to them. "I have lived with my characters, and thence has come whatever success I have obtained. There is a gallery of them, and of all in that gallery I . . . know the tone of the voice, and the colour of the hair, every flame of the eye, and the very clothes they wear." An author of integrity, he said, must keep such friends with him "as he lies down to sleep, and as he wakes from his dreams".

WHO'S WHO

Madeline Stanhope Dr Vesey Stanhope's crippled daughter who returns from Italy as Signora Neroni.

Obadiah Slope The new chaplain determined to reform Barchester. "New men are carrying out new measures," he says, "and are carting away the useless rubbish of past centuries".

Septimus Harding The former warden of Hiram's Hospital who becomes unwittingly involved in a power struggle between Slope and Mrs Proudie.

Eleanor Bold Harding's daughter, recently widowed and with a baby son.

Mrs Proudie The wife of the new bishop. "I cannot think", observes the author, "that with all her virtues she adds much to her husband's happiness".

Dr Proudie The new bishop of Barchester, dominated by his wife and swayed by the insinuations of Slope.

Dr Grantly The archdeacon and Harding's son-in-law, a worldly and forceful character, bitterly disappointed at not being made bishop.

Bertie Stanhope Dr Vesey Stanhope's son: a charming wastrel who is urged by his sister to marry Eleanor Bold for her money.

Mr Quiverful The rector of Puddingdale, hopeful of being offered the vacant post of warden at Hiram's Hospital.

Dr Francis Arabin Vicar of St Ewold, and contender for the post of Dean of Barchester. He falls in love with Eleanor Bold.

City of York Art Gallery/Bridgeman Art Library

Walker Art Gallery, Liverpool

Obadiah Slope (left) has mastered the art of being insinuating and offensive simultaneously. He blocks direct approaches to the bishop and claims to speak on his behalf. In effect, therefore, Slope rules supreme in Barchester, sharing power with Mrs Proudie until ambition and lust get the better of him.

Barchester gossips (right) are the audience before whom the drama unfolds. They are a group of parochial, conservative, opinionated but 'oh so respectable' ladies and gentlemen of the cathedral congregation. The old men of the Hospital also act as commentators on events.

Fine Art Photographic Library

The gentle Eleanor Bold (right) has the sweetness and conscience of her father, but her refusal to shun Slope makes her the subject of slanderous speculation.

"This lady is . . . authoritative to all, but to her poor husband she is despotic" (left). Mrs Proudie's desire for absolute power does not stop short at domestic matters. She fancies she knows best how to run the bishopric and fill the vacancy at Hiram's Hospital. Splendid in her tyranny, she grew into a character both loved and hated by Trollope's readers.

Madeline Stanhope (left) "a basilisk from whom an ardent lover of beauty could make no escape", holds naïve Barchester in thrall. Resplendent in the title of La Signora Vesey Neroni, she plays up her mysterious past and her disability with a mixture of cynicism and coquetry, thereby seeking to influence the outcome of events.

"Doubting himself was Mr Harding's weakness" (right). He wrestles with the new ideas of Slope and Mrs Proudie, trying to decide whether he or they are morally in the right. The reader is left in no doubt as to the truth – Septimus Harding speaks with the voice of the author and is condemned only for his timidity. Shyly talented at arranging music for the church and playing his violincello, Septimus is loved and respected by everyone, especially the old men at the Hospital. He dreads acrimony and arguments as much as the idea of being in the wrong. His worst dilemma comes when his beloved daughter seems to be involved with the abominable Slope.

LIVING CHARACTERS

With seemingly limitless powers of concentration, Trollope daily wrote for three and a half hours before breakfast – creating some of the most realistic characters in all fiction.

In his autobiography, Trollope asserts that he became a novelist because he was too poor and too badly educated to do anything else. 'I had often told myself since I left school that the only career in life within my reach was that of an author, and the only mode of authorship open to me that of a writer of novels.' Like many of Trollope's statements, this has to be taken with a pinch of salt. If novel-writing had been merely a common-sense choice, Trollope would have taken to it during his miserable early years in the Post Office. Yet it was only when he had married, and his work for the GPO had become more congenial and better paid, that he ventured on his first novel.

His industrious attitude to writing was probably inspired by the example of his remarkable mother. Frances Trollope had written nothing until she was over fifty, when financial desperation drove her to produce her famous *Domestic Manners of the Americans*. She went on to publish some 40 books – more than a hundred volumes – though her writing hardly impinged on the life of the family it supported: 'She was at her table at four in the morning, and had finished her work before the world had begun to be aroused.'

Her son followed a similar routine, rising at 5am and writing between 6am and 9.30. He worked with his watch placed on the desk in front of him, and aimed to produce 250 words every quarter of an hour – a grand total of 3500 words, written before breakfast and the beginning of his working day.

Nothing was allowed to disrupt Trollope's literary production. When his official duties involved extensive travel, he adapted himself to writing in trains. 'I made for myself therefore a little tablet, and found after a few days'

National Portrait Gallery, London

Travelling writer
'I passed in railway-carriages very many hours of my existence,' wrote Trollope, describing his days in the employ of the Post Office. 'I made myself therefore a little tablet, and found that I could write as quickly in a railway-carriage as I could at my desk.' Indeed, his practice of writing in trains became well known. This cartoon makes a snide reference to it when the Melbourne Punch *somehow misconstrued Trollope's writings about Australia as a slight on Australian womanhood.*

Bodleian Library, Oxford

Working to rule
(left) Trollope's working schedule for Barchester Towers. *His methodical working habits – revealed in his autobiography – shocked his readers. He wrote a huge quota of words each day, and if he finished a book and his daily quota was incomplete, he immediately began the next novel. Trollope considered himself 'just a shoemaker . . . only taking care to make honest stitches'.*

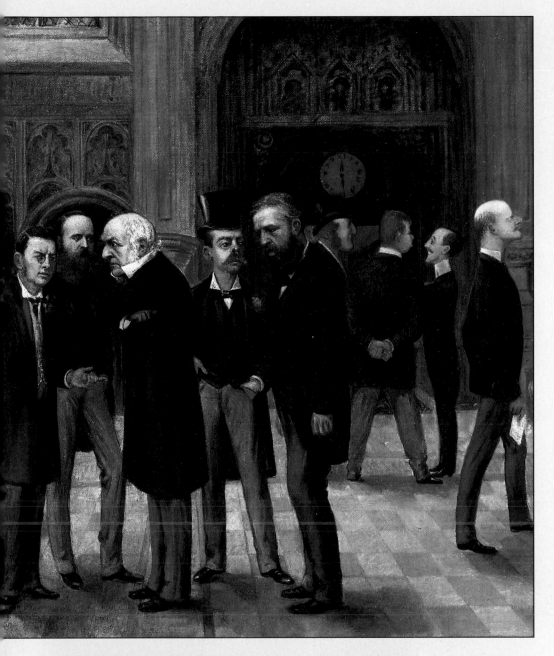

exercise that I could write as quickly in a railway-carriage as I could at my desk. I worked with a pencil, and what I wrote my wife copied afterwards. In this way was composed the greater part of *Barchester Towers*.'

Trollope even kept to his self-imposed schedules on ocean voyages, working steadily at his desk between violent bouts of sea-sickness. After his retirement from the Post Office, his routine changed a little – he rose later, and sometimes dictated rather than wrote. But he remained as strenuously productive as ever.

In this fashion, Trollope – for years a part-time writer – managed to become one of the most prolific and respected of all English authors. He published more novels – 47 – than the collective total produced by Dickens, Thackeray, George Eliot, Jane Austen and the Brontës. And although his ventures into drama and non-fictional social criticism may best be forgotten, his short stories and travel books remain highly readable.

Trollope himself believed that *The West Indies and The Spanish Main* (1859), about his voyage round the Caribbean, was the best of all his books. 'It is short and, I think I may venture to say, amusing, useful, and true.' Thanks to his working habits, it was also vivid – written during the actual voyage, without making a single note, before his immediate impressions had begun to fade.

THE GREAT SERIES

But it is for his Barchester and Palliser series that Trollope is best remembered. The Barchester Chronicles started with the publication of his fourth novel, *The Warden* (1855), a delightful book which sets the scene, depicting rural Barsetshire life and introducing some of the characters who reappear throughout the series. *Barchester Towers* (1857) followed, two years later, and then four more – *Doctor Thorne* (1858), *Framley Parsonage* (1861), *The Small House at Allington* (1864) and *The Last Chronicle of Barset* (1867).

The comedy of the Barchester Chronicles is replaced by a stronger sense of satire in the Palliser novels. These consist of *Can You Forgive Her?* (1864), *Phineas Finn* (1869), *The Eustace Diamonds* (1873), *Phineas Redux* (1874), *The Prime Minister* (1876), and finally *The Duke's Children* (1880). *Phineas Finn* and *Phineas Redux* represented, Trollope believed, 'a pessimistic view of triumph'.

Much of Trollope's writing is the result of observation of human behaviour and insight into what Henry James called 'the heart of man'. But his personal experiences and feelings also influenced the content of his novels. A financial catastrophe (such as had befallen his family) often threatens or occurs. Even some quite sensational fictional incidents in his novels had real-life equivalents: the episode of

Political series
After Trollope's unsuccessful excursion into real-life politics, his political instincts were expressed in a series now known as The Palliser novels. Politicians and the courts of power (above) fascinated him.

Irish inspiration
A ruined manor-house (left), glimpsed in Ireland is thought to have inspired Trollope's first novel – The Macdermots of Ballycloran.

Leeds City Art Gallery

43

the mislaid cheque in *The Last Chronicle of Barset*, for example, resembles an incident in Trollope's early life, when he was accused of stealing by his superior in the GPO, though in Trollope's case the matter was cleared up within a few minutes. More directly, the character and career of Charley Tudor in *The Three Clerks* are certainly based on those of the young, floundering Anthony Trollope. And the seedy lodgings and slightly disreputable dalliances of Johnny Eames, in *The Small House at Allington*, match what is known of Trollope's early career in London.

THE AFFECTIONATE CRITIC

Current issues also influenced Trollope. Among other things he attacked the new civil service examinations in *The Three Clerks*, and based the almshouse controversy in *The Warden* on a real contemporary scandal. But the setting of his first series – the county of Barsetshire and the cathedral city of Barchester – was an imaginative creation that went far beyond the initial impulse provided by Trollope's working tour of the south-west to reorganize postal deliveries.

The Warden reveals an imaginative sympathy that enables Trollope to feel the charm of a tradition he nonetheless believes must be abolished. The same sympathy is extended to his characters: 'In the writing of *Barchester Towers* I took great delight. The bishop and Mrs Proudie were very real to me, as were also the troubles of the archdeacon and Mr Slope.' In fact, despite his apparent produc-

tion-line mode of writing, Trollope was utterly committed to his work and characters. He insisted that 'the writer, when he sits down to commence a novel, should do so, not because he has to tell a story, but because he has a story to tell.' Above all, he must know his characters by living constantly with them. 'They must be with him as he lies down to sleep and as he wakes from his dreams. He must learn to hate them and love them. He must argue with them, quarrel with them, forgive them, and even submit to them.' Such dedication was what made Trollope's characters some of the most rounded, the most convincing in all literature.

The Palliser novels, though sparked by Trollope's frustrated political ambitions, owe more to creative insight than to experience. He became familiar with the ways of the House of Commons by sitting in the Speaker's Gallery, but Trollope's knowledge of behind-the-scenes politics and aristocratic circles – vital ingredients of the Palliser novels – must have been almost non-existent. Yet the books convinced readers then as they do now. Trollope himself thought that his 20th-century reputation might rest on his creation of three characters – the Reverend Mr Crawley (in *The Last Chronicle of Barset*), Plantagenet Palliser and Palliser's wife, Lady Glencora.

Trollope's reputation has undergone curious vicissitudes. During his lifetime, his novels were popular with the reading public and admired by writers as different as Thackeray, Nathaniel Hawthorne and Henry

James. But his work became a little unfashionable in his later years. And the publication immediately after his death of his *Autobiography* (1883) dealt a shattering, if unjust, blow to his reputation.

20TH-CENTURY REVIVAL

Strangely devoted to the myth of the great artist as a divinely driven figure, critics and readers were repelled by revelations that this author wrote by the clock, noted the income that each book brought him, and happily compared novel writing with the making of shoes. With this new perspective on Trollope, Victorian audiences were suddenly able to overlook the merit, the sheer genius of the work achieved under this arduous and businesslike regime. From being one of the most popular writers of his day, Trollope fell into disrepute and interest in his novels declined until a revival in the 1940s.

According to James Pope Hennessy, it was during World War Two that 'the sturdy realist of mid-Victorian England achieved a fresh fame as a leading writer of escapist literature.' His novels contrasted so dramatically with the realities of life in air-raid shelters that they engendered an overwhelming sense of nostalgia – a yearning for the solid, the ordinary and the predictable. And today, his reputation is as high as it has ever been. For his wit, perception and compassion – as much as for his vivid evocation of Victorian society – Trollope is one of the most widely read and enjoyed 19th-century novelists.

British Library, London/Bridgeman Art Library

Writing at sea
Trollope's best book, in his opinion, was The West Indies & the Spanish Main, *written during a voyage there.*

Robert H. Taylor Collection/Princeton University Library

Millais illustrations
The artist Millais illustrated many of Trollope's novels. This plate is from Framley Parsonage.

WORKS·IN OUTLINE

Trollope's literary output was so large (his novels alone number 47 and he wrote more than a dozen works of non-fiction) that no selection can do them proper justice. Henry James wrote that 'His great, his inestimable merit was his complete appreciation of the usual', and this perhaps explains the particular, enduring success of the 'Barsetshire' novels, all set in provincial England.

They begin with *The Warden* (1855). The classic *Barchester Towers* (1857) was the second in the series, followed by *Doctor Thorne* (1858), *Framley Parsonage* (1861), *The Small House at Allington* (1864) and *The Last Chronicle of Barset* (1867).

The Three Clerks (1858) is perhaps Trollope's most autobiographical work of fiction, *The Vicar of Bullhampton* (1870) his frankest, and *The Way We Live Now* (1875) his hardest hitting social satire.

In recent years, the reputation and popularity of Trollope's political novels has risen steadily, and some would claim the 'Palliser' series (1864–80) as the finest and most fulfilling of all his achievements.

THE BARCHESTER CHRONICLES
◆ 1855-67 ◆

Country church life (above) binds together the events and characters of these novels. *The Warden* introduces Septimus Harding, the mild man of principle who becomes a dilemma in the life of his daughter and son-in-law (left). A minor character *Dr Thorne* becomes the hero of the third book, when unforunate events surrounding the birth of his adopted daughter hamper the girl's romantic prospects. At *Framley Parsonage*, the Archdeacon, Dr Thorne and the Duke of Omnium (later to appear in the Palliser series) jointly observe the sad downfall of a country parson undone by ambition. *The Small House at Allington* concerns sisters Lily and Bell Dale and their choice of men. In *The Last Chronicle of Barset* many familiar faces re-emerge. Mrs Proudie takes arms against a vicar accused of theft, meets opposition from the Bishop, and then receives an even greater shock.

Fine Art Photographic Library

Mansell Collection

THE PALLISER NOVELS
✦ 1864–1880 ✦

The excitement and skullduggery of electioneering (right) brought Trollope no success as a politician, but as an author he made wonderful capital from it. The famous group of Palliser novels is set among Britain's ruling elite and gives a vividly accurate picture of parliamentary life. In *Can You Forgive Her?* (1864) the Duke of Omnium's son, Plantagenet Palliser, a dry man wrapped up in his political interests, marries the Scottish heiress Lady Glencora MacCluskie. But the Lady Glencora continues to dream of an earlier lover, the dashing Burgo Fitzgerald. In *Phineas Finn* (1869) Plantagenet wisely declines the opportunity to become Chancellor of the Exchequer in order to save his marriage. This book is mainly concerned with the political and romantic adventures of Phineas, a young Irishman who eventually gives up his career to marry his first sweetheart.

   The Eustace Diamonds (1873) is dominated by a fascinatingly wicked widow, Lizzie Eustace (right), who makes an unscrupulous attempt to hold on to a valuable family heirloom at all costs. To do so, she makes an injudicious second marriage, but *Phineas Redux* (1874) reveals her husband to be a bigamist. The book chronicles the return of Phineas who becomes an MP and survives a sensational murder trial.

   In *The Prime Minister* (1876), the Pallisers are again at the centre of events. Plantagenet, now Duke of Omnium, becomes Prime Minister, ably supported by Glencora. She overreaches herself, however, and causes a crisis that jeopardizes Palliser's government. The final volume, *The Duke's Children* (1880), sees Plantagenet a widower. 'The Prime Minister' appears as a racehorse, and a new generation of Pallisers are making their way in the world.

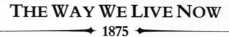

Bridgeman Art Library

THE WAY WE LIVE NOW
✦ 1875 ✦

Felix Carbury is not just a gambler (left), but a worthless fortune-hunter moving in circles which value money above any code of ethics. For Trollope's longest novel is an angry, satirical attack on London society for abandoning traditional values and blindly worshipping financial success. Financier Augustus Melmotte, who establishes himself in the city almost overnight by dispensing lavish hospitality, is rumoured to be immensely rich, and soon becomes a Conservative MP. Melmotte's illegitimate daughter, Marie, is courted by London's impoverished young men-about-town, and although Melmotte wants her to marry into the peerage, Marie falls in love with Sir Felix Carbury. The couple plan to elope with money stolen from Melmotte, but even before they leave, the foolish Carbury gambles it all away in a single night. The theft fatally weakens Melmotte's increasingly shaky position, and the financier's career comes to a spectacular climax. Felix is even less fortunate in a subsequent amorous adventure, and most of the novel's 'undesirables' eventually quit the country they have helped to corrupt.

Beraud: La Salle de Jeu. Musée Carnavalet. Giraudon/Bridgeman Art Library

Fine Art Photographic Library

Harris Museum & Art Gallery, Preston

THE THREE CLERKS
◆ 1858 ◆

Three clerks in the Civil Service (below), Henry Norman, Alaric Tudor and Alaric's feckless cousin Charley, become involved with the three daughters of a clergyman's widow, Mrs Woodward. The well-born Henry loves Gertrude Woodward, but she chooses to marry his friend Alaric – by no means a wise choice, for clever Alaric lacks principles. Alaric rises impressively through the Civil Service by means of the new-fangled competitive examinations that Henry so despises.

Under the influence of a distinctly shady Member of Parliament, Undecimus Scott, Alaric uses government money for unsound private investments. He is found out and goes to prison for embezzlement, despite the efforts of a great 'Trollopian' character, the lawyer Chaffenbrass. On his release, Alaric is helped to emigrate to New Zealand by Henry Norman who, having unexpectedly inherited an estate is now comfortably off and happily married to Gertrude's sister, Linda.

Meanwhile, likeable Charley Tudor's erratic career is dogged by debts and errors of judgement. But he is savèd by the devotion of the youngest Woodward sister, Kate. The crisis *he* has to face occurs when Katie is stricken with an apparently fatal illness.

Trollope's early working life at the Post Office and his comfortless, slightly wild life in seedy London lodgings, are clearly mirrored in the novel. Many of the experiences of Charley (who becomes a writer by sheer hard work and perseverence) have a particularly autobiographical flavour.

Fine Art Photographic Library

THE VICAR OF BULLHAMPTON
◆ 1870 ◆

Carry Brattle, seduced and abandoned in London, is forced to lead an increasingly disreputable life (left). She is the daughter of the Bullhampton miller, and her brother Sam is also in trouble, suspected of having murdered a Bullhampton farmer. A heartless local magnate, the Marquis of Trowbridge, demands the eviction of the entire disgraced family, but their landlord, Harry Gilmore, refuses to be bullied into agreeing.

When the vicar of Bullhampton, Frank Fenwick, supports Gilmore, the Marquis revenges himself by giving some land to the Primitive Methodists – an anathema to the Anglicans. To the vicar's horror, the Methodists use the land to build a chapel directly opposite the vicarage gates. Fenwick, however, succeeds in discovering the real murderer, in rescuing and securing forgiveness for Carry, and even in turning the tables on the Marquis and the Methodists.

Trollope wrote this novel 'chiefly with the idea of exciting not only pity but sympathy for a fallen woman'. The subject was too shocking for many of his readers.

The Postal Boom

From the Frank Staff Collection, on loan to Bath Postal Museum

The postal reforms of the 1840s and 50s ushered in a new era for the Post Office – postage was cheaper, services became more efficient and the number of letters mailed virtually tripled.

Trollope's energies were, for most of his life, divided between writing and his work for the Post Office. Despite a clash of personalities with his renowned but dour boss, Rowland Hill, he undoubtedly made great contributions to the organization of the national and international postal system. He is even reputed to have invented the pillar box. His lifetime spanned the single most vital period in the development of postal services, and although something of this was due to the calibre of such men as Trollope and Hill, advances came also in response to social change. During Trollope's life, Britain and its Empire were transformed from a group of isolated communities into an interdependent whole.

The news of Anthony Trollope's birth in 1815 would have been learned by relatives around the county by letter. The letters would have travelled by stage-coaches which sped night and day along Britain's great post-roads. The 17th century had seen the creation of the General Post Office – a public service under government control. The 18th century had seen a vastly improved road network and the system of 'post boys' on horseback replaced by stage-coaches. Every night, at exactly 8 o'clock, mail coaches left London for all parts of Britain. They were kept to schedule with the aid of time-pieces which could only be unlocked by supervisors at the various staging posts along their routes.

By 1797, 42 such routes were in operation. Journey times were kept to a minimum: 27 hours from London to Holyhead and 43 hours from London to Edinburgh. Everything was done to minimize delay. Teams of horses could be changed in two minutes. Village mail was dropped off and taken aboard without the coach even stopping. And despite this being the era of the highway robber, the mail coaches had a well-deserved reputation for efficiency, punctuality and reliability. There were still many grounds for complaint and aspects which cried out for improvement. Letters were paid for at the receiving end, and charged according to the number of sheets and the mileage that had been covered, which often proved to be uneconomic. Postage could cost less on a short letter going from London to Edinburgh than for a long

one going from London to Kent. Additionally, letters might be refused by their recipients, much as a reverse-charge phonecall might be refused today: then the letter had to be returned to sender without any recompense to the Post Office. The postal system did not seem to be keeping up with the needs of a modern, industrial economy. Another problem was that it favoured the weal-

Crown Copyright

Fine Art Photographic Library

The pillar box
(above) Based on an idea by Trollope, the pillar box was instituted in the 1850s. Prior to that, letters had to be taken to receiving stations or to 'bellmen' – roving, bell-ringing postmen.

Sir Rowland Hill
Disliked by Trollope, Hill (left), was an impassioned reformer whose commitment to improving the postal system bordered on an obsession.

The General Post Office
This crowded scene (above) shows the range of Londoners who rushed to catch the post just before closing time at 6 o'clock.

Post boys
(left) In the early 18th century letters were carried across the land on horseback. Progress was slow, riders were unarmed and robbery was commonplace. A Parliamentary Act of 1765 insisted that post boys should not loiter on the roads, nor 'wilfully misspend' their time, nor cover less than 6 miles an hour.

The Royal Mail
John Palmer, born in Bath in 1742, first suggested the use of stage-coaches for transporting mail. Mail coaches were duly tested in 1784 and proved an immediate success. With a team of four horses and an armed guard, the post was conveyed to its destination in safety and what seemed at the time remarkable speed.

thy. By reducing and standardizing postal rates, Hill envisaged social benefits as well as financial ones. The working class would be encouraged to keep in touch with friends and relatives by letter and consequently greater literacy would be fostered.

ROWLAND HILL
The man who mobilized public opinion and the government was (Sir) Rowland Hill. He was one of those extraordinary Victorian supermen, with interests including printing, astronomy, mathematics, transportation and taxation. In 1837 he privately issued a little book entitled *Post Office Reform: its Importance and Practicability* (officially published the following year). In it he suggested a blindingly simple system. Postage should be pre-paid, and letters should be charged by weight only. For a flat rate of one penny, letters of less than half an ounce should be carried anywhere inland. Such a cheap, uniform rate would mean more people would use the service, which would be cheaper to administer and so, in the long run, would not operate at a loss.

The Post Office should provide pre-paid envelopes and wrappers. But for those wishing to use their own stationery, he proposed 'a bit of paper just large enough to bear the stamp' (meaning the official Post Office hand-stamp) 'and covered at the back with a glutinous wash, which might, by applying a little moisture, attach to the back of the letter . . .' This was the origin of the Penny Black, the world's first adhesive postage stamp.

Backed by public enthusiasm, Rowland Hill was asked by the government to revamp the General Post Office. There he was much resented by the other officials (among them Anthony Trollope) who saw him as an outsider, a new broom whose appointment implied criticism of them. The tensions betweeen Hill and Trollope were particularly marked, for the novelist was by character as 'bluff and boisterous' as the reformer was 'calm and freezing'.

In his *Autobiography* Trollope discussed his relationship to Hill with characteristic frankness, 'With him I never had any sympathy, nor he with me . . . I was always an anti-Hillite, acknowledging indeed the great thing which Sir Rowland Hill had done for the country, but believing him entirely unfit to manage men or to arrange labour.'

Hill's reforms began to take effect. By May 1840 stamps, wrappers and envelopes were available to the public. Until the invention of an envelope-making machine in the 1850s, envelopes were an expensive lux-

49

ury. Nevertheless, contrary to expectation, it was the glutinous stamps bearing the young Queen Victoria's portrait which sold best. Printers worked night and day to keep pace with sales of the Penny Black: 66 million were produced before the colour was changed to red a year later.

Hill's trust in the popularity of a cheaper postal system was immediately vindicated. The number of letters posted in 1840 was double that of the year before. Government revenue fell, however, not to be redeemed for several decades.

By 1855 pillar boxes dotted the country, replacing the more expensive 'letter-receiving' offices which did the job first. If the pillar box was indeed Trollope's invention, it indicates how sincerely he did work for Rowland Hill's 'great thing' despite his dislike of the man. In 1870 the postcard – an innovation pioneered by the Austrians – was introduced, incorporating a half-penny stamp. It proved particularly popular in Scotland.

TRAINS AND SCHOOLS

Vital to the take-off of the new postal system was the integration of the Royal Mail with the expanding railway network. The last mail stage-coach left London in 1846, but letters had been carried on trains before the Penny Post – even as early as 1830. And the Penny Post coincided with Britain's 'railway mania'. By 1855, 8000 miles of track were in operation. Not only were trains faster than stage-coaches, they also afforded facilities for sorting the mail in transit.

In Trollope's Britain the very word 'railway' smacked of a new, ultra-modern way of life. The fact that the railways ran to a published timetable led to a nationwide synchronization of pocket watches: they could be set by station clocks which told the same time from one end of the country to the other.

WRITING HOME

The ability to communicate by letter became more important as Britain was transformed from a rural to an urban, industrial society. By the 1851 census, the urban population had overtaken the rural, and it was no longer common to die in the parish of your birth. Prime Minister William Gladstone considered that the Penny Post had a part to play in easing the pain of such migration as families separated in the search for work: 'Think what softening of domestic exile, what an aid in keeping warm the feel of family affection, in mitigating the rude breach in the circle of the hearth.'

As the postal system expanded, another major breakthrough in communication came with the telegraph. William Cooke and Charles Wheatstone had patented their method in the very year of Rowland Hill's influential book on Post Office reform. But it was an American, Samuel Morse, who gave his name to the most successful code. A British Electric Telegraph Company was set up in 1845, but by 1870 the Post Office had taken exclusive control of all the telegraph offices. The first cable between Britain and France was laid in 1850, between Britain and America in 1866, and

Envelope-making machine
(right) The advent of stamps and the reform of postal rates, led to another popular innovation – the envelope.

American links
(below right) In 1868 Trollope went to America to negotiate an international postal treaty. By 1881, 25 per cent of Britain's overseas mail came from there.

Sea mail
Overseas letters were transported in two ways – on private vessels and on government or Post Office ships. The picture right shows a post office aboard a private vessel, the steamer 'Pekin'.

The iron horse
(below) The building of an efficient rail network presented another opportunity for the Post Office. Letters began to be carried by train in 1830 and by 1838 mail trains were equipped with travelling post offices on board. Travel times were approximately 20 miles an hour.

De La Rue Co., London/Bridgeman Art Library

New York State Historical Association, Cooperstown

between Britain and Australia, via Singapore, in 1871.

Women were associated with telegraphy from the outset. When the Post Office took over, it was decided to permit women telegraphists. This had nothing to do with emancipation. It simply reflected the fact that the GPO could not do without them. The story goes that the Chairman of the London Electric Telegraph Company heard of a stationmaster's daughter who had been ably carrying out all of her father's telegraph duties for several years. Soon the Company found that 'the girls are not only more teachable, more attentive, and quicker-eyed than the men clerks', but also 'sooner satisfied with lower wages'.

These female telegraphists underwent far more rigorous scrutiny of their abilities and characters than the young Anthony Trollope had done in 1834. The age of patronage, old-boy networks and class snobbery died with the introduction in 1870 of competitive examinations. for recruitment to the Civil Service in general. The same decade saw 'gentlewomen of limited means' employed as Post Office clerks for the first time. Fears about the impropriety of 'the admixture of the sexes' proved unfounded. On the contrary, it was seen to raise 'the tone of the male staff by confining them during many hours of the day to a decency of conversation and demeanour which is not always to be found where men alone are employed'.

OVERSEAS MAIL

The Penny Post, the telegraph and the railways shrank Britain, and the rest of the world was shrinking too. Railways wound their way across continents, and steam ships ploughed the oceans. Other governments were quick to imitate Britain's cheap, pre-paid system of postage. In the spring of 1868, Trollope went on a special mission to America to negotiate a postal treaty. Although a 'far from agreeable' mission, on account of the offhand inefficiency of one American official who offended the novelist 'grievously', it was successful. The year 1874 saw the setting up of an International Postal Union whose members agreed to place their inland postal systems at the disposal of all others, and to pool information about improvements.

The colonies, in particular, enjoyed excellent com-

munication facilities, so that administrators and armies could be quickly contacted by the motherland, and emigrants could keep in touch with families at home.

Trollope had retired before the next round of revolutionary advances in the Post Office. These can largely be attributed to Henry Fawcett who, in four short years as Postmaster General (1880–1884), made the Post Office counter central to daily life. He introduced six major new services: the parcel post, postal orders, sixpenny telegrams, savings stamps, and annuity and insurance schemes. (The habit of thrift he encouraged had a social effect. Urban workers tended to marry rather than cohabit, since a post-office nest-egg could not be left to a common-law spouse.)

In 1885, the postman (a word coined only in Fawcett's time) traded his penny-farthing for a 'safety bicycle'. He must have cut a figure rather akin to the lone and long-gone 'post boy'. But behind him now towered a monumental organization of a vast labour force, technology and bureaucracy – a General Post Office indispensable to the social and economic maintenance of country and Empire.

Barnaby's Picture Library

Cheap labour
The Post Office was a pioneer in the employment of women, but it was for economic motives rather than progressive ones. Women could be paid less than men, and tended to be more efficient and better educated than their male counterparts. In 1897, 33 per cent of telegraphists and over half the counter clerks were female, and there was an agreement that one-third of the staff at the Central Telegraph Office (above) would be female. A condition of employment was that the women would resign on marriage. This served to keep their salaries low since they would rarely stay long enough to be promoted.

Crown Copyright

'Hen and Chickens'
Aptly nicknamed, this bicycle (left) was introduced in 1881 to help with parcel deliveries, but did not catch on. Bicycle postmen, in general, were expected to cover between 26 and 28 miles a day.

OSCAR WILDE

◆ 1854-1900 ◆

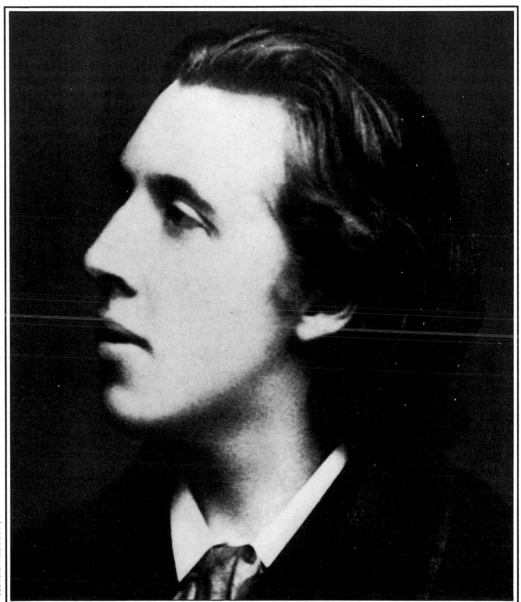

BBC Hulton Picture Library

'Somehow or other I'll be famous, and if not famous, I'll be notorious,' declared the young Oscar Wilde: he proved to be both. From the moment he burst upon fashionable society he was a celebrity, fêted for his dazzling wit and affectionately mocked for his 'poetic' nature and flamboyant behaviour. But the world in which Wilde moved was riddled with hypocrisy – hypocrisy which Wilde relentlessly exposed. And when his celebrity turned to notoriety, the society that had so flattered him was merciless.

Fame and Infamy

Brilliant, flamboyant and with quicksilver wit, Oscar Wilde was the darling of late Victorian society – until he transgressed its intractable moral laws.

One of the most gifted and most often quoted users of the English language was an Irishman by blood, birth and upbringing. Oscar Wilde lived and conversed much in the style of his writing, alternately shocking and captivating the London society he had chosen for his audience. 'I've put my genius into my life,' he said at the end, 'only my talent into my works.'

Oscar Fingal O'Flahertie Wills Wilde was born on 16 October, 1854 at 21 Westland Row in Dublin, the second son of remarkable parents. His father, Sir William Ralph Wills Wilde, was a leading eye and ear surgeon, a scholar of some repute and a noted archaeologist.

Oscar's mother was even more of a celebrity than his father at the time of their marriage. Under the pen-name 'Speranza', Jane Francesca Elgee, Lady Wilde wrote passionate nationalistic articles for the radical newspaper, *The Nation*, and was an ardent advocate of women's rights. She exerted a powerful influence over her second son's life. 'All poets love their mothers', Wilde later said, 'I worshipped mine.' And she called him 'best and kindest of sons'.

THE FUTURE SCHOLAR

Oscar's childhood was happy and carefree, his parents indulgent and loving. Like most boys of his class, aged 10 he was sent to a public (private) school – Portora Royal, near Enniskillen. Although a bookish boy, Oscar did less well academically than his elder brother Willie, but at the age of 16 he developed a passionate interest in the classics, particularly Greek, at which he excelled. In the autumn of 1871 he entered Trinity College, Dublin, where he

An Irish upbringing
(above) Wilde was born in Dublin, into a titled, talented and somewhat eccentric family. He studied Greek at Trinity College Dublin – winning a scholarship to Oxford at the age of 20.

Dramatic mother
(far left) 'Speranza', Oscar Wilde's mother was a profound influence on her son. She was a well-known Irish Nationalist and poetess (though not a very good one). After marrying in 1851, she became the focal point of Dublin's literary circle. Oscar adored her.

A gifted father
(left) Sir William Wilde, Oscar's father was a famous, gifted surgeon. He had three legitimate children and several illegitimate ones. Like Oscar, he was at the centre of a highly publicized and scandalous trial – when he was accused of molesting one of his patients. (He won the case.) He is seen here exhibiting his notorious and eccentric scruffiness.

won the Berkeley Gold Medal for Greek and in 1874 a scholarship to Magdalen College, Oxford.

'I was the happiest man in the world', exclaimed Wilde, 'when I entered Magdalen for the first time'. He spent four idyllic years at Oxford. Already noted for his brilliant conversation and boldness of dress, Wilde cultivated his taste for the finer things of life. Indeed, as he was to say later, he sometimes felt that his life was one long struggle against stupidity and dullness – vices to which he felt the English were particularly addicted. He left Oxford in 1878. Armed with a double first (best possible degree), the Newdigate Prize for English Verse and the reputation of an eccentric genius, he set out to take London by storm – 'I'll be a poet, a writer, a dramatist. Somehow or other I'll be famous, and if not famous, I'll be notorious'. In the years that were to follow, Oscar Wilde was to be each of these things in turn.

Installing himself in Thames House, Salisbury Street, Wilde began cultivating dandyism and became known as the 'apostle of aestheticism'. During this period of his life, Wilde would do anything to be seen and talked about. "There is only one thing in the world worse than being talked about", he wrote in *The Picture of Dorian Gray*, "and that is not being talked about." He became the talk of the town, his wit, charm and audacity making up for a lack of proven literary accomplishment.

Key Dates

1854 born in Dublin
1871 goes to Trinity College, Dublin
1874 goes to Magdalen College, Oxford
1878 graduates with a double first
1881 *Poems* published
1882 American lecture tour
1884 marries Constance
1891 meets Lord Alfred Douglas. *The Picture of Dorian Gray* published
1895 *The Importance of Being Earnest* performed. Sentenced to two years hard labour at Pentonville and Reading jails
1897 writes *De Profundis*. Goes to live in France
1898 writes *The Ballad of Reading Gaol*
1900 dies in Paris

The young Oscar
(left) Wilde, aged two, in a velvet dress. Although some writers have made much of this mode of dress in relation to Oscar's homosexuality, it was customary among the upper classes to dress young boys in what is now considered 'girls' clothing'.

Magdalen College
(above) Wilde spent four years at Oxford. He was a brilliant classical scholar, gaining a 'double first' (the highest possible grade of degree) and the Newdigate Prize. Armed with academic success, he intended to take London by storm.

He dressed in a way calculated to shock. His rich velvet coats, knee-breeches, stockings, flowing ties and buckled shoes upset the Victorian gentleman's sense of decorum. His pose was languishing and highly sensitive. Once, asked what he had done all day, he replied, 'I was working on the proof of one of my poems all the morning, and took out a comma. In the afternoon I put it back again.'

SAVED BY PATIENCE

His sayings and doings very soon became the subject of savage satire in *Punch*, but it was Gilbert and Sullivan's comic operetta, *Patience*, that gained him national notoriety. A skit on aestheticism, it was taken to be an attack on Wilde, who nevertheless found it highly amusing. But notoriety did not pay the bills. In an attempt to make some money Wilde published his *Poems* in July 1881. Condemned by critics for their lack of originality, the poet's preoccupation with physical beauty and the bodily grace of boys also raised eyebrows. But happily for Wilde the public showed sufficient interest for the volume to run into five editions.

Ironically, however, it was *Patience* that really saved Wilde from penury. After its success in Britain, the D'Oyly Carte Company decided to take the production across the Atlantic. But for the operetta to be understood it was felt necessary to explain what English 'aestheticism' was. And who better to perform the task than Oscar Wilde himself? Accordingly, on Christmas Eve 1881, Wilde set sail for the New World. Spending almost a year in America, he travelled from coast to coast, and made over 50 personal appearances and a great deal of money.

Returning to Europe, he stayed only briefly in London before moving on to Paris. Here, apart from enjoying café life, he wrote a play, *The Duchess of Padua*, for the American actress Mary Anderson who, on receiving it, promptly turned it down. This

set-back forced him to look for another source of income. Back in London in May 1883, Wilde again signed up for a lecture tour – of the English provinces.

Bored by the prospect of lecturing even before the tour began, Wilde nevertheless turned up for the opening night at Wandsworth Town Hall on 24 September and stayed with it to the end at Crystal Palace on 5 March. His repertoire consisted of three talks: 'The House Beautiful', 'The Value of Art in Modern Life', and 'Personal Impressions of America'. As always his physical appearance at first threw his audience – the long locks of earlier years now replaced by a curled 'Neronian coiffure' – but his rich melodious voice and ready wit soon had them all laughing heartily.

Wife and child
(below) Wilde met the beautiful Constance Lloyd in Dublin. They married in 1884, and set up home in Chelsea. The couple had several happy years together, and two children – Cyril (pictured here with his mother) and Vyvyan.

American success
(left) New York was the scene of Wilde's first major public performance. He arrived on 2 January 1882 – ahead of the touring opera Patience, in order to explain its subject, English aestheticism, to the Americans.

On arriving in the United States, the customs query 'Have you anything to declare?' gave Wilde the opportunity to reply 'Nothing but my genius'. The Americans could hardly believe what they saw (Oscar in velvet breeches and floppy ties), let alone what they heard. They treated him as a joke, but his lecture tour drew vast crowds and made him a fortune.

Mansell Collection

At the Royal Academy
(above) Wilde soon became a famous sight in fashionable London. Seen here at the Royal Academy in 1881, he attracted as much interest as the paintings – probably more. But as yet, his fame greatly exceeded his wealth.

In November he was in Dublin where he met and fell in love with Constance Mary Lloyd, who attended his lectures. They had met two years previously and felt a deep attraction for each other. They were married on 29 May 1884. Within a year, a son, Cyril, was born, to be followed by another boy, Vyvyan, the following year. The couple set up home in Tite Street in Chelsea, transforming an ordinary terraced house into 'The House Beautiful'. But Wilde did not have the income to pay for everyday domestic needs, or the extravagant lunches he indulged in at the Café Royal.

Wilde therefore embarked on yet another lecture tour before taking up book reviewing for the *Pall Mall Gazette*. And in June 1887 he became the editor

'The House Beautiful'
Wilde transformed his house in Chelsea into 'The House Beautiful' – with exquisite decorations and works of art.

of *The Lady's World*. Changing the title to *The Woman's World*, Wilde enlarged its format, introduced colour on to the front page, and shifted it up-market with articles on literature, art and society. Though circulation increased, Wilde soon tired of it, and his appearances in the office dwindled to a few hours a week, until he resigned in 1889.

If the role of a diligent editor was one which he found irksome, that of family man was even more difficult. After two years of happiness, Wilde grew increasingly bored with his wife and disillusioned with marriage. He developed a close relationship with a 17-year-old ex-Cambridge undergraduate, Robert Ross – a relationship that was to last until Wilde's death.

RISE AND FALL

Wilde's reputation as a major writer rests on the work he produced within a period of seven years, beginning with children's stories including *The Happy Prince* in 1888, and culminating in *The Importance of Being Earnest* in 1895. During these seven years, Wilde experimented with almost every literary form, from short stories to comic drama.

Lady Windermere's Fan, a 'modern drawing-room play with pink lampshades', was first produced at St James's Theatre in February 1892. On the first night Wilde himself appeared on the stage after the performance had ended to rapturous applause. 'Ladies and Gentlemen', he said, 'I congratulate you on the great success of your performance, which persuades me that you think almost as highly of the play as I do.'

By 1895 he had two plays running in the West End and more money coming in than ever before. Wilde was now at the pinnacle of success and good

Fact or Fiction

THE ORIGINAL PORTRAIT

There are two possible sources for the idea of Dorian Gray and his portrait. One is that Wilde himself, following a sitting for the artist Frances Richards, looked at his own image and remarked 'What a tragic thing it is! The portrait will never grow older, and I shall. If it was only the other way!'

Another version involves an unknown sitter for the artist Basil Ward. Wilde saw an extremely beautiful young man at his studio and lamented that such a 'glorious creature should ever grow old'. Ward agreed, saying 'How delightful it would be if he could remain exactly as he is while the portrait ... withered in his stead'.

Roy Miles Gallery/Bridgeman Art Library

The original 'Basil' *of the story may have been the artist Basil Ward.*

WILDE VERSUS QUEENSBERRY

The Marquess of Queensberry was out to get Wilde from the day he discovered that he was a close friend of his son, Lord Alfred Douglas. Queensberry even burst into Wilde's home accusing him of 'disgusting conduct'. Shortly after, he accused Wilde of being a sodomite (homosexual). Reckless Oscar immediately took him to court for libel.

The trial became a battle between Queensberry's counsel, Edward Carson, and Wilde. Carson probed; Wilde defended wittily, but he was eventually lacerated by his own cleverness. When asked if he had kissed a certain boy, he replied, 'Oh, dear no. He was a peculiarly ugly boy'. And what, Carson damningly inferred, if he had been beautiful?

Wilde's case was blown. From this moment on events went Queensberry's way. After dropping the case, Wilde himself was arrested on charges of indecency. This trial ended in stalemate; the third resulted in Wilde's prison sentence. It virtually killed him.

him, and when it became clear that the Defence had assembled witnesses to prove the justification of Queensberry's claim, Wilde was advised to drop the case. This he did, but instead of leaving the country as everyone advised him to do, he drove to lunch, and on to Bosie's room at the Cadogan Hotel. That evening, Wilde was arrested. The next day he was transferred to Holloway Jail.

Wilde's trial began on 26 April at the Old Bailey. He was charged on 25 counts of gross indecency, and conspiring to procure the commission of acts of indecency. After four days, during which there was a succession of paid witnesses in the box, the jury

fortune. But an incident, in itself insignificant, set in motion a train of events that would bring him ruin.

In 1891 he had developed an obsession for Lord Alfred Douglas, the 21-year-old son of the Marquess of Queensberry. Douglas possessed three qualities which Wilde found irresistible – youth, beauty and a title. In fact, like his 'mad' father, Lord Alfred ('Bosie') was arrogant, wilful, self-indulgent, indiscreet and vengeful. His relationship with Wilde was tempestuous, and soon became common gossip.

Flushed with success, Wilde did little to hide his passion, dining in public and holidaying abroad with Bosie, much to the wrath of Queensberry. Having hounded Wilde for months, threatening to shoot him if he saw him with Bosie in public, on 18 February 1895 Queensberry left his visiting card at Wilde's club, the Albermarle, with the misspelt message 'For Oscar Wilde posing as a somdomite (sic)'.

It would have been safer to ignore the insult, but instead Wilde issued a writ for libel against Queensberry who was duly arrested and charged on 2 March. Assuring counsel that there was no truth in Queensberry's allegation, Wilde was convinced of a favourable verdict. Entering the Old Bailey on 3 April, Wilde played to a packed courtroom. His performance when cross-examined by Sir Edward Carson was masterly.

But on the second day, things did not go so well. Questioned about a certain Alfred Taylor (who kept a disreputable house which Wilde frequently visited), his answers were, as he admitted, 'absurd and silly perjuries'. Pressed by Carson he became evasive and frankly horrified when he realized the amount of evidence Queensberry had amassed against him. He remained self-assured but his answers became damningly revealing.

The feeling of the court was now turning against

Oscar and Bosie

Oscar Wilde met Lord Alfred Douglas (seated) in 1891. Douglas was a striking, spoilt undergraduate who was captivated by Wilde's brilliance. And Wilde, in turn, fell for his 'red rose-leaf lips' and 'slim gilt soul'. The friendship led to Wilde's trial and imprisonment. After, when Wilde had been released and was living in exile, Douglas visited him in France. The always difficult relationship ended when Wilde asked his extremely wealthy friend to lend him some money. The irrational Douglas flew into paroxysms of rage and soon returned to England. They never met again.

Avents Collection, New York Public Library

Mansell Collection

retired to consider its verdict. To everyone's surprise, and the judge's obvious irritation, they failed to reach a verdict. On 1 May the case was dismissed and four days later, Wilde was released on bail.

Still, despite the pleading of friends, Wilde refused to flee the country. Consequently on 20 May another trial opened at the Central Criminal Court before Mr Justice Wills. The same ground was covered again, but this time Wilde was found guilty on all but one count and received the sentence of two years hard labour.

Wilde served the whole of his sentence. The first five months were spent at Pentonville in conditions of unrelieved horror. For speaking to another prisoner he was placed in solitary confinement in total darkness for 24 hours. Conditions improved marginally when he was moved to Reading Jail, though he considered he was treated cruelly. His spirit, once so lively and joyous, and his always-precarious health were soon broken.

In the two years he spent in prison, Wilde wrote a long and bitter letter to Lord Alfred accusing him, with good reason, of having caused his downfall. Called *De Profundis* by his literary executor Robert Ross, the letter was only published in its entirety in 1962. Intensely personal, it contains some of the most beautiful of his prose.

EXILE IN FRANCE

After his release on 19 May 1897, Wilde lived out the remainder of his life in France, an exile, 'broken-hearted, ruined, disgraced, a leper and a pariah to men'. In that time, he wrote just one major work, *The Ballad of Reading Gaol*, which was to be his last and finest poem.

After a temporary reconciliation with Bosie, his 'dear boy', the two parted never to meet again. Lack of money and loneliness were his major preoccupations. Constance had divorced him and changed her name before she died prematurely in 1898, and Wilde was forbidden to see either of his sons. He drank heavily. When warned that drinking would kill him, he retorted 'And what have I to live for?' But to a small circle of friends his conversation could be just as lively, good-humoured and witty as ever. Crippled with illness, he continued to joke, saying, 'I am dying, as I have lived, beyond my means'. And of the paper on the wall of his bedroom, he said, 'It is killing me. One of us *has* to go'.

On 30 November 1900 he died of cerebral meningitis, at the age of 46. He had already been received into the Roman Catholic Church and on 3 December was buried at Bagneux.

Prison drudgery
(below) This contemporary engraving illustrates the appalling degradation and meaningless activity that Wilde endured during his two years' hard labour. He served his full term, and lost his spirit and his health.

Mary Evans Picture Library

Fall from grace
(right) With his self-conscious pose and distinctive looks, Wilde had always been a target for caricature. This cruel example shows the once graceful aesthete leaving for France in shame.

Mansell Collection

THE PICTURE OF DORIAN GRAY

**Wilde's only novel is the devastating story of an elegant young man corrupted
by decadence and sin. He remains eternally young and beautiful, but his
portrait reveals his true age and hideous nature.**

One of the most shocking novels of a generation, and one which was to play a part in Wilde's downfall, *The Picture of Dorian Gray* combines sparkling wit, social satire and indulgently luxurious description with doom-laden intensity. Holding these elements together is the central brilliant idea of parallel lives – one lived by the eternally youthful and apparently pure Dorian Gray, the other by the fateful portrait which bears the burden of his age and sins.

Wilde's mastery of the witty, paradoxical epigram and quick-fire dialogue make the novel a joy to read, yet its subject is a fundamentally tragic one of a soul's wilful descent into evil.

GUIDE TO THE PLOT

In the London studio of the wealthy painter Basil Hallward, the air is filled with "the rich odour of roses" and "the heavy scent of lilac". On a "divan of Persian saddle-bags" lies old-Etonian Lord Henry Wotton, Basil's friend from their Oxford days, smoking a "heavy

> "'How sad it is! I shall grow old, and horrible, and dreadful. But this picture will remain always young... If it were I who was to be always young, and the picture that was to grow old!... I would give my soul for that!'"

opium-tainted cigarette" and admiring Basil's latest "portrait of a young man of extraordinary personal beauty".

Basil admits that it is a portrait of a new acquaintance named Dorian Gray, who obsesses him and inspires his art. He is unwilling to introduce Dorian to the elegant, cynical and fascinating Lord Henry, but is forced to do so when the young man arrives for a sitting. Flippantly turning aside Basil's entreaties not to corrupt Dorian's "simple and beautiful nature", Lord Henry sets out to exert his charm and influence.

Fateful inspiration
Basil's artistic obsession with Dorian's beauty sets the story in motion. His portrait is an increasingly ugly reminder of the corruption beneath the appearance of purity.

Death of an actress
Sybil rejects the artifice of acting for the reality of love, but Dorian leaves her, saying: "Without your art you are nothing". Unmoved by her tragic suicide, he views it only as "a wonderful ending of a wonderful play".

Dorian Gray is rapidly converted to the "New Hedonism" preached (but not necessarily practised) by Lord Henry, who encourages him to indulge every whim and be "always searching for new sensations", telling Dorian, with characteristic wit, that "The only way to get rid of a temptation is to yield to it".

Lord Henry also makes Dorian aware of the impermanence of his youth and beauty – "a sharp pang of pain went through him like a knife, and made each delicate fibre of his nature quiver. His eyes deepened to amethyst, and across them came a mist of tears" – and

Fine Art Photographic Library

National Portrait Gallery, London

James Tissot: Hush. City of Manchester Art Galleries

B. Marchal, Paris/Giraudon/Bridgeman

Glittering gatherings
Dorian's public life revolves around the salons and soirées given and attended by the rich, glamorous, leisured classes.

Secret pleasures
When Dorian was not mixing with high-society, he sought out London's low-life and "sordid sinners" to extend his experience.

gazing at his life-like portrait, Dorian suddenly utters the wish that the painting could grow old instead of him, leaving him untouched by time. He says he would give his soul for it.

Under Lord Henry's influence, Dorian goes in search of new experiences and begins to explore the murky areas of London. In a shabby little theatre, he sees and falls in love with Sybil Vane, an exquisite young actress, who gives superb performances as Juliet and other Shakespearian heroines. They become engaged. Sybil's younger brother, a sullen young sailor swears that if her "Prince Charming", as she calls Dorian, harms her, he will kill him.

When Dorian takes Basil and Lord Henry to see Sybil act, he is stunned by the mediocrity and artificiality of her performance. She proudly explains that now she has known real love she sees through "the hollowness, the sham, the silliness of the empty pageant", but Dorian's feelings are just the opposite. He loved the artist in Sybil and her ability to realize "the dreams of great poets", and now feels only contempt for the "third-rate actress with a pretty face". He brutally rejects her anguished attempts to win him back.

Returning home, he finds that his portrait has altered subtly – "there was a touch of cruelty in the mouth". He realizes with horror that his "mad wish that he might remain young, and the portrait grow old; that his own beauty might be untarnished, and the face on the canvas should bear the burden of his passions and his sins" has come true.

Having been made aware of his sin, Dorian resolves to do good, and marry Sybil. But it is too late – the next morning he learns that she has killed herself, and he is easily persuaded by Lord Henry to take a pleasurably

aesthetic, spectator's view of her death: "It has all the terrible beauty of a Greek tragedy".

Locking away the tell-tale portrait in a disused room, Dorian plunges into a life of scarlet, unnamed sins. A "poisonous book" lent to him by Lord Henry adds to the evil influences on him, and encourages his over-indulgent pursuit of sensual pleasure. Eighteen years pass – "Summer followed summer, and the yellow jonquils bloomed and died many times, and nights of horror repeated the story of their shame, but he was unchanged. No winter marred his face or stained his flower-like bloom". But rumours abound about his mysterious disappearances to the "foulest dens in London" and his "fatal" friendships with young men.

When Dorian stoops to murder and blackmail, the by-now hideous portrait almost oozes blood. His fashionable, aristocratic friends know nothing of his secret, and only Sybil Vane's brother can threaten him.

"A poisonous book"
Lord Henry sends Dorian a novel in which "The life of the senses was described in terms of mystical philosophy". This "poisonous book" which encourages Dorian's pursuit of sensations and sin was based on A Rebours (Against Nature) by the decadent writer J.K. Huysmans. The model for Huysmans' 'hero' was Robert de Montesquiou (right).

Yet Dorian is increasingly haunted by the loathsome "image of his sin", and makes a last attempt to reform himself by sparing a village girl he might have seduced. But when he looks for some sign of improvement in the portrait, he finds instead "in the mouth the curved wrinkle of the hypocrite". The picture is, by now, both his conscience, and the evidence against him. Determined to destroy it, he picks up a knife – and in a sensational outcome, poetic justice is done at last.

MORAL OR IMMORAL?
When *The Picture of Dorian Gray* appeared in *Lippincott's Monthly Magazine* in 1890 it was stridently condemned as immoral. 'It is a tale spawned from the leprous literature of the French *décadents* – a poisoned book, the atmosphere of which is heavy with . . . moral and spiritual putrefaction', wrote the critic from the *Daily Chronicle*.

British Library/Musée d'Orsay/Réunion des musées nationaux

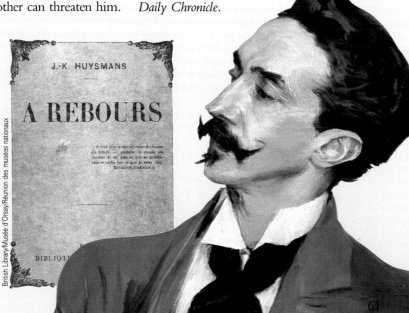

J.-K. HUYSMANS

A REBOURS

BIBLIOT

Oscar's reply to the Press was as witty and cutting as the novel itself: 'The poor public, hearing, from an authority so high as your own, that this is a wicked book that should be suppressed, will no doubt rush to read it. But alas! they will find that it is a story with a moral. And the moral is this: All excess, as well as all renunciation, brings its own punishment. Yes, there is a terrible moral in *Dorian Gray* – a moral which the prurient will not be able to find in it, but which is revealed to

> "*Eternal youth, infinite passion, pleasures subtle and secret, wild joy and wilder sins – he was to have all these things. The portrait was to bear the burden of his shame: that was all.*"

all whose minds are healthy.' But when the story was published in book form, he toned down some of the apparent references to homosexuality, and added a conventional melodramatic sub-plot (James Vane's revenge) to appease the critics.

Despite Wilde's half-flippant, half-serious assertion in the novel's Preface that "There is no such thing as a moral or an immoral book. Books are well written, or badly written. That is all.", the story of the pursuit of evil, leading ultimately to damnation, is a stark one. It is the modern equivalent of the medieval legend of Faust, the man who sold his soul

Darkest London
Having committed murder, Dorian seeks oblivion in the dark back streets and opium dens of London's dockland, which he has frequented for 18 years. Leaving the exquisite luxury of Lady Narborough's drawing room, he dresses "commonly" and takes a hansom to the East End: "Over the low roofs and jagged chimney stacks of the houses rose the black masts of ships. . . The slimy pavement looked like a wet mackintosh".

Atkinson Grimshaw: Goodbye at the Gate/Fine Art Photographic Library

to the devil for a year of unlimited power. As a woman Dorian has ruined says "he has sold himself to the devil for a pretty face".

Part of the problem in the Victorian 'misunderstanding' of the book is that Wilde made Dorian's sins appear so attractive. When Dorian reads the "poisonous" book which Lord Henry gives him, "It seemed to him that in exquisite raiment, and to the delicate sound of flutes, the sins of the world were passing in dumb show before him". And Wilde's own prose makes decadence sound seductive.

But as Lord Henry pointedly remarks, "Beautiful sins, like beautiful things, are the

privilege of the rich". Many rich Victorians could afford to indulge such sins even though they apparently lived a spotless existence: "we are in the native land of the hypocrite", "The books that the world calls immoral are books that show the world its shame".

Dorian leads the double life of a Victorian gentleman, in an exaggeratedly evil form. On the surface, he is an aristocratic man–about–town, but also frequents sordid opium dens near the docks, prey to "mad hungers that grew more ravenous as he fed on them". His portrait is an emblem of the hypocrisy of such a life as well as a "monstrous soul image".

E.J. Gregory: A Duet/Fine Art Photographic Library

Society flirtations
Eternally youthful good looks make Dorian a favourite with society ladies such as the pretty, flirtatious Duchess of Monmouth. She attends a party at Dorian's country home where Sybil's brother James catches up with him at last.

A shooting accident
Dorian's house guests are enjoying an afternoon's shooting, when their day is marred by one of them accidentally killing James who is hiding in a thicket. "It would not look well to go on" is the callous, well-bred response.

J.M. Ten Kate: The Game 'Hunters/Fine Art Photographic Library

Wotton's "wilful" paradoxes and polished epigrams could easily have been delivered by Wilde himself, and probably were. For like Wotton, Wilde would play with an idea and use it in various versions whenever the opportunity arose in life or in art. Some of Wotton's witticisms even appear in adapted form in Wilde's plays – "one of those characteristic British faces, that, once seen, are never remembered", and "when her third husband died, her hair turned quite gold from grief".

Wilde envied Dorian's beautiful looks and youth – "youth is the only thing worth having", as Lord Henry says. But although he headed the aesthetic 'cult of Beauty', he was also aware of aestheticism's superficiality, and of the desperation which coloured its decadent excesses. Dorian's lust for eternal youth and beauty leads him to sin and ugliness, until he recognizes that "It was his beauty that ruined him, his beauty and the youth he prayed for. But for those two things, his life might have been free from stain. His beauty had been to him but a mask, his youth a mockery".

Throughout the novel there is a sense of fatality about where Dorian's lifestyle must lead him – perhaps reflecting Wilde's feelings about the inevitable consequences of his own way of life. Writing to Bosie from the prison cell that was to be his eventual fate, he refers to this as the "Doom that like a purple thread runs through the gold cloth of *Dorian Gray*". And it is this sense of doom and despair – heightened by contrast with the glittering surface wit – which gives the story its compelling moral force.

The emotional force with which Wilde writes probably owes much to his own experience of a similar double life - as a married society man and covert homosexual. Like Dorian, once the rumours of his clandestine activities had spread, Oscar had to endure occasional snubs in drawing rooms and clubs, when he too must have "felt keenly the terrible pleasure of a double life".

During Wilde's trial the supposedly autobiographical elements of the novel, particularly the veiled hints of homosexuality, were quoted against him. And many critics have identified Wilde with the witty, corrupting Lord Henry. But Wilde declared: 'Basil Hallward is what I think I am: Lord Henry what the world thinks of me: Dorian what I would like to be – in other ages, perhaps'. But he desired Dorian's youth and beauty.

REAL-LIFE PARALLELS

There are, indeed, elements of all three men in Wilde. He was an artist, like Basil, inspired by an abstract sense of Beauty. And Lord Henry's languorous pose and cruel, epigrammatic wit – "you would sacrifice anybody, Harry, for the sake of an epigram" – certainly reflect Wilde's public persona.

| In the Background |

OPIUM DENS

Opium was in popular use centuries before Dorian Gray sought out "opium dens, where one could buy oblivion". For much of the 19th century, the drug was perfectly respectable, especially in its liquid form, laudanum, which was widely available as a painkiller. Many people used it habitually. Later, as Dickens' *The Mystery of Edwin Drood* and Wilde's *The Picture of Dorian Gray* reveal, opium became associated with "dens" in Limehouse and other parts of London's dockland.

In the public mind, the Limehouse Chinese were identified as the 'villains' of the drug traffic – ironically so, since it was the British who had introduced opium into China and encouraged the lucrative drug trade.

Squalid drug dens sprang up throughout the docklands of Victorian England.

Mary Evans Picture Library

CHARACTERS IN FOCUS

The glittering main characters of *The Picture of Dorian Gray* are typical products of the upper echelons of late-Victorian society, drawn together both to satirize that society and to play their role in the novel's wider moral purpose. At the centre of the web of characters is Dorian himself, worshipped by Basil, corrupted by Lord Henry, and destroying most people he meets – from the naïve actress Sybil Vane to the briefly glimpsed Adrian Singleton, society-man turned pitiful opium addict.

WHO'S WHO

Dorian Gray A beautiful, rich, spoilt young man, aged about 20 at the start of the story. His pure good looks belie his increasing age and sinfulness.

Basil Hallward An artist. Obsessed and inspired by Dorian's beauty, he paints the fateful portrait of him.

Lord Henry Wotton Basil's elegant, cynical and irresistibly witty friend, who encourages Dorian's life of self-gratification, but never guesses where the "New Hedonism" he preaches has led his young protégé.

Lady Henry His wife – "she tried to look picturesque, but only succeeded in being untidy".

Lord Fermor Lord Henry's uncle, who indulges "the great artistocratic art of doing absolutely nothing" – usually at his club.

Sybil Vane An exquisitely beautiful, gifted young actress with whom Dorian falls in love when he sees her act.

James Vane Her gruff-mannered younger brother. He goes to sea, and returns 18 years later.

Mrs Vane Their mother – "a faded, tired woman who played Lady Capulet in a sort of magenta dressing-wrapper".

Lady Narborough An elderly society hostess – "a very clever woman with . . . the remains of really remarkable ugliness".

Duchess of Monmouth A pretty, witty, bored young woman, married to "a jaded-looking man of sixty".

Alan Campbell A brilliant scientist who shares an unnamed secret with Dorian Gray.

H. de Callas: An Elegant Soirée/Fine Art Photographic Library

Titled characters exchange bitchy gossip, but accept Dorian despite "whispered scandals" – revealing the hypocrisy of "civilized society". Their group "feels instinctively that manners are of more importance than morals, and . . . that the highest respectability is of much less value than the possession of a good *chef*".

Louis Huvéy: The Rake/Fine Art Photographic Library

"Prince Paradox", Lord Henry Wotton is a charming, aristocratic, affected but cynical dandy. After arriving late ("punctuality is the thief of time"), he has a tendency to fling himself upon sofas or into chairs and deliver cutting, paradoxical epigrams, then "smoke a cigarette with a self-conscious and satisfied air, as if he had summed up the world in a phrase". With his "romantic, olive-coloured face and worn expression", his "low, languid voice", "cool, white, flower-like hands", and "wrong, fascinating, poisonous, delightful theories . . . about love [and] pleasure", he enjoys exerting his irresistible influence on Dorian. His friend Basil Hallward says to him: "You never say a moral thing, and you never do a wrong thing", and although Lord Henry likes to preach that "one could never pay too high a price for any sensation", it is his beautiful "creation", Dorian Gray – not himself – who lives his pleasure-seeking philosophy, and pays for it.

Whitford & Hughes, London/Bridgeman Art Library

J.M. Aiken: Portrait of the artist. Spink & Son Ltd/Michael Simpson/Bridgeman Art Library

"The loveliest thing I had ever seen in my life" – "all the great heroines of the world in one" is how Dorian describes Sybil Vane. Only 17, she "knows nothing of life", but is an inspired actress. Her love for Dorian destroys her ability to act – and so Dorian rejects her.

***"A young lad. . . thick-set of figure"*,** James Vane is jealous and suspicious of Sybil's rich admirer. He asserts melo-dramatically that "if this man wrongs my sister, I will find out who he is, track him down, and kill him like a dog". He returns from Australia 18 years after Sybil's death to fulfil his threat.

Christie's, London/Bridgeman Art Library

"Yes, he was certainly wonderfully handsome, with his finely-curved scarlet lips, his frank blue eyes, his crisp gold hair. There was something in his face that made one trust him at once. All the candour of youth was there, as well as all youth's passionate purity. One felt that he had kept himself unspotted from the world. No wonder Basil worshipped him." This is Lord Henry Wotton's first impression of Dorian Gray when he arrives for a portrait sitting at Basil Hallward's studio. Despite his "wilful, petulant manner", Dorian's good looks initially reflect a pure, good nature. But Basil and Lord Henry make him aware of his own beauty and its impermanence, and Dorian utters a wish that the portrait which Basil has just painted of him could age in his place, so that he could always retain his youthful beauty. The wish is granted. When Dorian plunges into a life of decadent self-gratification and indulgence which leads him sin, the portrait not only ages in his place, but reflects the real image of his corrupted soul.

"Basil . . . puts everything that is charming in him into his work . . . Good artists exist simply in what they make, and consequently are perfectly uninteresting in what they are". Basil Hallward is talented and dedicated as a painter, and a loyal friend. But his adulation of Dorian's beauty has fatal consequences.

Aberdeen Art Gallery and Museums

A PROFOUND WIT

Oscar Wilde delighted Victorian society with his scintillating wit and genius for epigrams, but behind the sparkling façade lay a serious purpose, and in his major works laughter is underlined with tragedy.

Of all the great Victorian writers, few were even half as versatile as Oscar Wilde. His only work as a novelist was *The Picture of Dorian Gray* – a remarkable first novel. But there was scarcely another kind of writing at which he did not try his hand. Poems, short stories, reviews, plays, fairy tales, even prose poems, seemed to flow from his pen with almost prodigious ease.

Wilde himself was both amused and pained by those who suggested that his very range suggested superficiality. In his play *Lady Windermere's Fan* (1892), Lady Windermere asks the languid, worldly Lord Darlington, "Why do you talk so trivially, then?" and the Lord amiably replies, "Because I think that life is far too important a thing ever to talk seriously about". Similarly, Wilde deflated those around him who were pompous enough to expound at length on life, while showing that behind his own flamboyant façade was a very serious man indeed.

Wilde was a cynic with a passionate belief in life, an idealist who played the role of disillusioned, world-weary lounge lizard. And in his mature works, high seriousness and high comedy go hand in hand.

Wilde's final prose work was a long letter written to Lord Alfred Douglas from Reading Jail and later published under the title *De Profundis* ('from the depths'). It is a tragic, intensely moving piece in which he lays bare his past and bitterly blames 'Bosie' for his downfall. Yet even of this dark work, the playwright George Bernard Shaw commented, 'There was more laughter between the lines of that book than in a thousand farces by men of no genius'.

But it was many years before Wilde perfected the mixture of showy wit and serious purpose that is the hallmark of his greatest work – although by all accounts he achieved it effortlessly in his conversation. Some of his earlier works are marred by the sententious, moralizing tone which he later condemned in the Preface to *The Picture of Dorian Gray*: "An ethical sympathy in an artist is an unpardonable mannerism of style".

SHAPING A TALENT

It was the discipline of writing for a living that pointed Wilde in the direction of his first real literary success. In the late 1880s, when his main income came from writing reviews and editing *Woman's World*, Wilde began to write short stories and essays succinctly, quickly and with less ornamentation. The results were wonderfully simple and direct. Some of these stories are simple yarns, like *Lord Arthur Savile's Crime* and *The Canterville Ghost*. But the most memorable are his charming fairy tales, such as *The Happy Prince*

J.S. Wells: Crowd Outside the Theatre. Christie's, London/Bridgeman Art Library

Illustrated London News

Mander and Mitchenson Theatre Collection

The drama of real life
(above) Rejecting Victorian melodrama, Wilde satirized his audiences, and created drama out of everyday society life.

Wilde on tour
Wilde knew how to woo an audience with his lectures – such as the 1882 tour of America – long before he wrote his best plays.

Mander and Mitchenson Theatre Collection/London Library

Theatre-goers
(left) Fashionable theatre-goers flocked to see The Importance of Being Earnest *and* An Ideal Husband *in the spring of 1895 and were delighted to see people like themselves portrayed on stage, larger than life and conversing with true Wildean brilliance. Perhaps many appreciated how deftly Wilde was exposing the sham of Victorian morality. But after cheering at night, the audience could read in the morning paper of the trial that was to destroy him.*

Literary pedigree
(below) In the late 1880s, Wilde began to prove that he could write – as well as dazzle with his conversation – by editing and writing articles for The Woman's World *magazine, and writing an enchanting series of fairy tales, four of which were collected in* A House of Pomegranates.

the price of everything and the value of nothing" – were noted and quoted as eagerly as any poetry.

Much of Wilde's brilliant conversation was natural and spontaneous. But he devoted a great deal of energy to perfecting his technique. Some of his most famous epigrams were probably not conceived spontaneously, but prepared in advance, with all the care of a playwright, to drop into the conversation at the right moment. Certainly, he was always listening out for good lines to save up for future use – which naturally led to accusations of plagiarism. When the artist Whistler, another famous wit, delivered a brilliant quip, Wilde remarked, 'I wish I had said that,' and Whistler replied pointedly, 'You will, Oscar, you will.'

There was such an element of performance about Oscar's social appearances that it was natural that his real literary genius should lie in writing for the stage. His gift for epigrams, his natural theatricality, and his unrivalled knowledge of fashionable conversation were the perfect raw material for plays. Even his novel *The Picture of Dorian Gray* has a theatrical element to it, and the languid dandified Lord Henry Wotton delivers epigrams with a flourish, almost as if anticipating applause from an audience beyond the footlights.

and the touching *The Fisherman and his Soul*. The clarity with which these tales bring out a moral – usually connected with love and self-sacrifice – foreshadow the moral framework of his great mature works.

But if these stories revealed Wilde's literary talent, it was into his conversation and his lectures that he poured his true genius. The salons and drawing rooms of London thrilled to his brilliant conversation and flashing wit. Admirers, especially women, would gather around him, hoping to be entertained. He rarely let them down.

His speciality was the 'epigram', of which he was an acknowledged master. Cultivated Victorian society loved epigrams – pointed, often ironic statements which wittily summed up an idea in a neat, perfectly poised sentence or two. Wonderful Wildean epigrams, delivered in his melodious drawl – such as "Experience is the name everyone gives to their mistakes", "Work is the curse of the drinking classes", and "A cynic is a man who knows

A character like Wotton appears in each of Wilde's social comedies, *A Woman of No Importance*, *Lady Windermere's Fan*, *An Ideal Husband* and his masterpiece *The Importance of Being Earnest*, delighting audiences with neat paradoxical epigrams and flashing wit, just as Wilde himself delighted fashionable society.

But these plays are much more than simply

vehicles for Wildean wit; they have a serious, even tragic, purpose. And they were highly – almost dangerously – original. At the time, theatre was stilted and hide-bound by stereotypes of melodrama, with predictable plots, and conventional morals. Wilde sought to throw out such conventions and reveal the bigoted Victorian society as it really was.

Wilde's plays were peopled by the same fashionable members of society who occupied the best seats in the theatre. They spoke the same language, attended identical house parties and displayed the same manners, albeit polished by Wilde's pen. By involving the audience in the emotions and reactions of the plays, Wilde achieved something that had been missing from the English stage for more than a century – a biting social satire.

CHALLENGING SOCIETY

But he went further than this. In each of the plays, Wilde's sympathetic treatment of women's roles is marked. In Mrs Allonby in *A Woman of No Importance*, for instance, Wilde created a woman as worldly and as witty as any of his male characters – and one who is quite prepared to put down men. When Lord Illingworth complains, "All women become like their mothers. That is their tragedy." Mrs Allonby replies, "No man does. That is his." Men in the audience were astonished, but women were delighted, for Wilde seemed to be challenging basic Victorian attitudes.

Indeed, Wilde challenged the whole Puritanical, heartless nature of Victorian society and tried to reveal the dangerous, cruel hypocrisy that was at the root of their attacks on pleasure, and by implication on love.

Wilde's greatest triumph, *The Importance of Being Earnest*, is often referred to as a light comedy of manners. Wilde himself described it as 'a trivial comedy for serious people'. But those familiar with his epigrammatic style knew that this indicated an enormous seriousness of intent. The play is a technical *tour de force*, based on classical farce, but with a powerful philosophical message.

Mary Evans Picture Library

The 'divine' Sarah
(above) Wilde believed that Sarah Bernhardt was 'undoubtedly the greatest artist on any stage' and was overjoyed when she agreed to star in the London première of Salomé. *But the play was banned by the Lord Chamberlain (left), (caricatured interviewing Wilde). Bernhardt appeared in the Paris version.*

Through the familiar doublings, mistaken identities, and impossible coincidences of farce, Wilde orchestrated the underlying theme that people really are who they pretend to be. And the hysteria as characters begin to lose control of their identity mirrors a society on the brink of great change as fossilized Victorian values began to crack. At the end of the first performance, the audience must have left entertained, but disturbed.

According to Wilde's friend Richard le Galliene, 'he made dying Victorianism laugh at itself, and what serious reformers had laboured for years to accomplish he did in a moment with the flash of an epigram; gaily, with humour and wit for his weapons'.

WORKS·IN OUTLINE

Oscar Wilde was famous as a brilliant wit and raconteur long before he made his name as a writer. But in the late 1880s, he entered a brief, remarkably creative period which saw him write nearly all the works still read and performed today.

He began by writing short stories, including the beautiful fairy tales in *The Happy Prince and Other Tales* (1888) and the thrillers, *Lord Arthur Savile's Crime and Other Stories* (1891). But after completing his single novel, *The Picture of Dorian Gray* he discovered his real genius in writing for the stage, beginning with the exotic *Salomé* (1891) and then embarking on the marvellous quartet of comedies, from *Lady Windermere's Fan* (1891) to his greatest masterpiece *The Importance of Being Earnest* (1895).

But this golden period was brought to an abrupt end by the disaster of Wilde's trial and imprisonment. After his release from prison, his only work of fiction was the powerful and tragic *Ballad of Reading Gaol*, written in exile and completed two years before he died.

Atkinson Grimshaw: Knostrop Hall/Fine Art Photographic Library

LORD ARTHUR SAVILE'S CRIME AND OTHER STORIES

→ 1891 ←

Canterville Chase provides an eerie setting (above) for Wilde's tale of *The Canterville Ghost*, the hilarious story of an American family living in an English house haunted by a lonely and incompetent ghost. All the stories in this collection are deliciously light-hearted, with an appealing touch of mystery and melodrama, and Wilde's genius for comedy shines through. In *Lord Arthur Savile's Crime*, the humour is black, as Lord Arthur searches for a murder to commit (right) to fulfil a palmist's grisly prediction; in the end it is the palmist he kills. In *The Sphinx without a Secret*, the comedy centres on a lady with a passion for mystery, while *The Model Millionaire* shows that wealth cannot be judged by appearance alone. They are as entertaining today as they were in Wilde's day.

City of Manchester Art Galleries

THE HAPPY PRINCE AND OTHER TALES

◆ 1888 ◆

The Happy Prince (right) is the bejewelled statue in the title story of Wilde's enchanting collection of fairy tales, first published with illustrations by Walter Crane and Jacomb Hood. Touching and sad, the story tells of how the statue, with the aid of a swallow, gives his gold and jewels to the poor; when all has been given away, the swallow dies and the statue is melted down. Like all the tales, *The Happy Prince* is beautiful simply read aloud, but it is also a passionate attack on a society which values Beauty above human happiness. *The Nightingale and the Rose* poignantly shows how love can be thrown aside, in the tale of the nightingale who sacrifices her life's blood to turn a white rose red for a lovelorn student, while *The Selfish Giant* who banishes children from his garden (below) is finally redeemed by his kindness to a little boy. Although he was inspired by contemporary children's writers, Wilde wrote these delightfully simple, but profoundly moral tales for readers of all ages.

Kent Collection

By permission of Gerald Duckworth & Co Ltd/ Mary Evans Picture Library

SALOMÉ

◆ 1891 ◆

Salomé's gruesome reward (left) for performing the erotic dance of the seven veils for her lustful stepfather, Herod, is the severed head of Jokanaan (John the Baptist), the imprisoned prophet who rejected her passionate advances. But Herod bitterly regrets agreeing to this terrible reward and, when Salomé frenziedly kisses the lips of the dead head, he orders her death. When Wilde first tried to stage this exotic and controversial play in London – written originally in French – it was banned by the Lord Chamberlain, for transgressing a centuries-old law forbidding the portrayal of biblical characters on stage. But the tragedy of *Salomé* is now recognized as a masterpiece. It is a dark, lush, almost operatic play, rich in sensuality and laden with doom, and was partly inspired by the equally ornate and sensual work of the artists Wilde met in Paris. For the first English translation (by Lord Alfred Douglas) of *Salomé* (1894), Aubrey Beardsley drew some spectacularly decadent illustrations, including a title page considered so obscene by the publishers that it was dropped (right). The German composer Richard Strauss created the operatic version.

Mary Evans Picture Library

Mansell Collection

LADY WINDERMERE'S FAN

✦ 1892 ✦

Lord Darlington's rooms (below) are the scene for the climax of Wilde's scintillating comedy of manners, his first London success. The play concerns the naïve, moralistic young Lady Windermere who becomes convinced of her husband's infidelity with the dubious Mrs Erlynne – really her mother who she believes dead – and tries to take comfort, and revenge, in a liaison with the worldly Lord Darlington. Trapped in Lord Darlington's rooms, she is saved in the nick of time by Mrs Erlynne who willingly sacrifices her own honour. The play ends happily with Lady Windermere, and the audience, wiser and more tolerant. Wilde described *Lady Windermere's Fan* as 'one of those modern drawing-room plays with pink lampshades' and the sparkling wit and brilliant epigrams delighted contemporary audiences. But beneath the glittering façade lay a penetrating attack on Victorian morality.

Mander and Mitchenson Theatre Collection

THE IMPORTANCE OF BEING EARNEST

✦ 1895 ✦

Jack Worthing proposes to Gwendolen Fairfax (below) while pretending to be his wild younger brother Ernest in order to have fun in town with his friend Algernon. Jack and Algernon are the two endearing young bachelors committed to pleasure in this, Wilde's most assured and successful play. The increasingly elaborate deceptions, or 'Bunburying', of the pair provide the classic elements of farce that drive the plot along. They are perfectly complemented by the two girls, Gwendolen and Cecily Cardew, but it is the monstrous and hilarious Lady Bracknell, one of the great comic creations of the English stage, who dominates the action. The brilliant conversation, dazzling wit and string of wonderful Wildean epigrams in *The Importance of Being Earnest* have delighted audiences ever since the opening night, when Oscar assured a reporter, 'The play *is* a success. The only question is whether the first night's audience will be.' But the play is much more than just a frothy comedy written, as Wilde claimed, 'by a butterfly for butterflies'; it is a sharp social satire with a profound message, revealed by Jack who discovers that he is who he pretends to be after all.

Franz Masereel © DACS 1

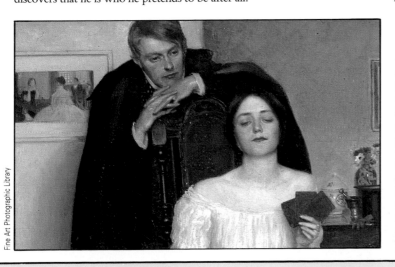

Fine Art Photographic Library

THE BALLAD OF READING GAOL

✦ 1898 ✦

C.3.3. was the alias under which Wilde originally published this long and bitter poem, written shortly after he was released from Reading Jail. C.3.3. was Wilde's own prison number, and the poem was inspired by his experience in the jail, and a hanging he witnessed there. The *Ballad* tells the story of a guardsman, convicted of murdering his lover, who awaits execution in the prison, watched balefully by the other convicts as he is exercised in the prison yard. As the fateful time draws near, the convicts are driven to despair by the thought of the doomed man in their midst. Then, at eight one morning, after a night of terrible anticipation, the condemned prisoner is hanged, and buried immediately in an unmarked grave – filled with quicklime to destroy the body hastily. The narrative is stark and simple, and the insistent song-like rhythm gives the *Ballad* an almost hypnotic power. The effect is one of the most moving indictments of capital punishment and the inhumanity of the penal system ever written, and it is justly Wilde's most famous poem.

Art and Decadence

Worshipping Beauty and cultivating the ideal of 'art for art's sake', the languid young aesthetes of Wilde's set adopted a decadent, sensation-seeking lifestyle that shocked High Victorian morality.

A s the 19th century drew to a close, a new mood could be felt among the writers and artists, poets and painters of England – a mood captured perfectly in *The Picture of Dorian Gray*. There was no cohesive 'movement' nor even a common philosophy – just a new spirit, known variously as 'aestheticism', 'decadence' or simply *fin de siècle* (end of century). But the ideas and personalities linked to this mood became, in the popular mind at least, synonymous with anything that was perverse, paradoxical or shocking. And of all the personalities associated with aestheticism, none was seen as more perverse, paradoxical and shocking than Oscar Wilde.

"LANGUID BEAUTY"

Writing in the 1890s on the contemporary aesthete's passion for beautiful things, the writer Max Beerbohm noted in an essay entitled *1880* that 'Beauty had existed long before 1880. It was Mr Oscar Wilde who managed her debut. To study the period is to admit that to him was due no small part of the social vogue Beauty was to enjoy'.

The vogue for 'Beauty' was first seen in the opulent taste in furnishings, fabrics and decor. Dados (elaborate friezes), peacock feathers, willow-pattern blue china, "sinuous draperies and unheard-of greens", all owed something to the aesthetic tastes of Mr Oscar Wilde. But Wilde's influence extended far beyond the home; aesthetes owed him something of their personality too. Beerbohm observed amusedly, 'Into whatever ballroom you went you would find, among the women in tiaras and the fops and the distinguished foreigners, half a score of ragamuffins in velveteen, murmuring sonnets, posturing, waving their hands'.

Wilde, in turn, owed something of his self-conscious posturing to the new 'dandyism' imported from France. There it had been made fashionable by the fiction of Theophile Gautier, whose *Mademoiselle de Maupin* (1835) came to be known as the 'Bible of the decadents'. The French author J. K. Huysmans' scandalous *A Rebours* is likely to have been the book Dorian Gray receives from Lord Henry Wotton, while Charles Baudelaire's *Les Fleurs du Mal* provided Wilde with a sense of "lurid and languid beauty".

Comic value
(right) Gilbert and Sullivan's comic opera of 1881, Patience, *lampooned Wilde and his ideas. The public delighted in mocking 'aesthetic' poetry, and its practitioners – a trend that publishers of sheet music were quick to cash in on.*

BBC Hulton Picture Library

Identifying with disaster
(right) The Decadents were obsessed with tragedy, and were inspired by the deathly beauty of classical, divine disasters. Many were to die tragically young themselves.

Gustave Moreau: Les Prétendants. Musée Gustave Moreau, Paris/Lauros-Giraudon

Aubrey Beardsley
*(left) Emaciated, affected,
but a brilliant success at 21,
Beardsley personified
decadent ideas and
behaviour, rivalling Wilde
for his notoriety.*

The Café Royal set
*(below) Ernest Dowson
was one of several doomed
poets belonging to the 'tragic
generation'. A member of
Wilde's set and of the
Rhymer's Club (which
included W. B. Yeats,
Lionel Johnson and Richard
Le Gallienne) he and his
mentors gathered in The
Café Royal (bottom), in
London's Piccadilly.*

BBC Hulton Picture Library

National Portrait Gallery, London

Charles Ginner: The Café Royal/Tate Gallery, London

French dandyism meant more than wearing extravagant dress; it was a complete lifestyle, based upon cultivating artifice and rejecting all that was merely commonplace and useful. "The first duty of life is to be as artificial as possible", echoed Oscar Wilde, on the other side of the Channel, a generation later. In place of solid Victorian 'virtues' of diligence, duty and prudence, the dandy favoured indolence, extravagance and self-indulgence.

Life was a perpetual pursuit of new sensations, and the decadent dandy in both France and England – cultivated, affected and refined – experimented with drink, drugs and sex in a way that was frankly shocking to contemporaries. Oscar Wilde may not have paraded down Piccadilly clutching a lily; it was sufficient (as he himself said) for people to believe that he had.

Later, in the late '80s and early '90s, Wilde's innocent lily gave way to an artificially coloured green carnation, the emblem of Parisian homosexuals. By habitually wearing one in his buttonhole, he combined artifice with the hint of forbidden pleasure.

ART AND MORALITY

The aesthete's flagrant disregard for middle-class morality was considered deeply subversive at the time. Their attitude to art was considered especially unsavoury. For most Victorians 'art' was a serious business with a moral purpose. To write as Wilde did in his Preface to *The Picture of Dorian Gray* that "There is no such thing as a moral or an immoral book. Books are well written or badly written. That is all", seemed to be an attack upon the foundations of society itself.

In fact, there was nothing new in this view at all. Gautier had written of *l'art pour l'art* (art for art's sake) more than half a century before *Dorian Gray*. In England, the idea had already been expressed by the painter James Whistler who stated that 'Art should be independent of all clap-trap – should stand alone, and appeal to the artistic sense of eye or ear, without confounding this with emotions entirely foreign to it, as devotion, pity, love, patriotism and the like'. And earlier in the century, the poet John Keats had written *Ode on a Grecian Urn* which contained the line, 'Beauty is truth, truth beauty'.

What Wilde did was to develop the idea into a coherent view of life. To Wilde, "The artist is the creator of beautiful things", and as such above ordinary moral judgements. Since art had nothing to do with morality, the artist was quite literally "beyond good and evil". When Wilde finally appeared in court on charges of homosexuality, it was not just his sexual morals that were being judged but also the idea of 'art for art's sake', and those who subscribed to it.

For the English aesthete, life revolved around the Café Royal in London. Wedged between Piccadilly and Glasshouse Street, it was *the* meeting place of the 'new' artists, writers, poets, musicians and wits. Here Oscar Wilde held court every day from one o'clock onwards and the eager voice of the emaciated painter Aubrey Beardsley could be heard above the general din, disclaiming 'Oh, really! How perfectly sweet!', 'Perfectly enchanting!' or 'Perfectly filthy!'. Beardsley, a success at the age of 21, in some ways rivalled Wilde as the personification of decadence and shared Wilde's sense of humour, once declaring that he had caught a cold by 'leaving the tassel off his cane'.

To the Café Royal, too, came many more of Wilde's set including the scruffy, tubercular poet Ernest Dowson, who died at the age of just 33. 'Poor wounded wonderful fellow that he was,' wrote Wilde when he died, 'a tragic reproduction of all tragic poetry, like a symbol, or a scene. I hope bay-leaves will be placed on his tomb, and rue, and myrtle too, for he knew what love is.'

Closely associated with the Café Royal set was the Rhymer's Club, whose members included the poet and critic Lionel Johnson who on initially meeting Wilde confessed to a friend, 'I am in love with him'. Also members were Arthur Symons (another poet and critic associated with literary decadence), John Gray (one of Wilde's young, 'precious' poets), and the young Irish poet W. B. Yeats. 'For some years', wrote Yeats, the Rhymer's Club met 'every night in an upper room with a sanded floor in an ancient eating-house in Fleet Street called the Cheshire Cheese.'

The aesthetes, thought Yeats, belonged to a 'tragic generation'. But their decadence was romantic rather than genuinely subversive. Although they wrote about prostitution – a common feature of London streets, but ignored by most 'establishment' writers – their attitude was muted and sentimental, with Symons writing about 'chance romances of the streets' and 'Juliet of the night'. Even homosexuality – a common interest among many members of the Club – was treated demurely, with Lord Alfred Douglas referring to it in a poem as 'The love that dare not speak its name' – a line which Wilde was to defend passionately and eloquently at the Old Bailey.

THE END OF AN ERA

To later generations, the spirit of the decadence was symbolized by *The Yellow Book*. This quarterly review of the arts first appeared in April 1894 with a drawing on the front cover by Beardsley, the quarterly's art editor. At the outset it seemed corrupt and dangerous, but after the first few issues *The Yellow Book* settled down to become a 'safe' publication, with regular contributions from Henry James, Edmund Gosse and George Sainsbury – all conservative writers. And with the trials of Oscar Wilde in 1895, *The Yellow Book's* publishers, The Bodley Head, panicked and sacked Beardsley, the most conspicuous 'decadent' member of staff. When Arthur Symons departed shortly afterwards, the publication became very tame indeed. Wilde himself was dismissive of it, saying that it was 'horrid', 'loathsome' and 'dull'. But since he was not asked to contribute, this criticism may not have been impartial.

Within a year of leaving *The Yellow Book*, Symons and Beardsley brought out a rival publication called *The Savoy*, which stood more courageously for the ideas and art of decadence. It was published by Leonard Smithers, purveyor of erotica, a regular at the Café Royal and a man considered so disreputable by W. B. Yeats, a contributor, that he refused to meet him. *The Savoy* lasted just one year and, apart from articles and drawings from leading 'decadents' (including an ultra-decadent 'romance' written by Aubrey Beardsley called *Under the Hill*), it published pieces from Bernard Shaw,

G. Klimt: Pallas Athene/Museen der Stadt Wien

Mansell Collection

Naughtiness and sin
(above) Beardsley's illustrations were associated with, and came to be used by, the decadent writers of The Café Royal set. His tailpiece to Wilde's play Salomé typifies his style and the content of many of his drawings – the clean lines depicting sensual nakedness, sinfulness and luxuriousness.

The Yellow Book
(left) Its art editor and illustrator was Aubrey Beardsley and, at the outset, it seemed to be the mouthpiece for the corrupt ideas of Decadence. But The Yellow Book – a quarterly arts review published by The Bodley Head – soon degenerated into a safe conservative publication as the 'movement' began to wane.

Mansell Collection

Symbolic details
(left) Decadent ideas owed much to European artistic influences, particularly the French and Austrian symbolists. In Gustav Klimt's strangely haunting portrait of the ancient Roman goddess of Wisdom, Pallas Athene, the dense mixture of mysticism, eroticism, classical detail and eerie opulence creates the effect that decadent authors sought to achieve in their writing.

Joseph Conrad, Lionel Johnson and Ford Madox Hueffer (later and better known as Ford Madox Ford).

The Savoy was only half the price of *The Yellow Book*, and was banned by the booksellers W. H. Smith, because it contained in one issue a reproduction of a drawing of a nude by William Blake. But it failed because, with Wilde in prison, 'decadence' was on the wane. The last issue in 1896 was written single-handed by Arthur Symons, who put the magazine's demise down to the fact that 'Comparatively few people care for art at all, and most of these care for it because they mistake it for something else'.

As a group of writers the 'decadents' have not survived. Little of what they produced is read today. Their literary style – following guidelines laid down by Gautier as 'ingenious, complex, learned, full of shades of meaning' – today seems too pretentious and wordy. In the fashion set by the pre-Raphaelite poet and artist Dante Gabriel Rossetti, the decadent writer would spend hours hunting out obscure, archaic and unusual words. His style was stilted, overblown and very artificial – failings not shared by Oscar Wilde.

Decadence did not outlast the death of the old cen-

Maxwell Armfield: Faustine. Musée d'Orsay, Paris/Giraudon/Bridgeman

Languid 'beautiful people'
(left) Maxwell Armfield's homage to the poet Swinburne, depicts the refined elegance and the world-weariness associated with the spirit of 'fin-de-siècle'. The furnishings and decoration in the room are scrupulously detailed in oriental, classical and allegorical imagery – the lily (shown wilting) was one of many flower emblems that came to symbolize the 'foppishness' of the aesthetic movement.

By courtesy of the Board of Trustees of the Victoria and Albert Museum

tury, nor did it survive Oscar Wilde's. 'In 1900', wrote W. B. Yeats, 'everybody got off his stilts; henceforth nobody drank absinthe with his black coffee; nobody went mad; nobody committed suicide; nobody joined the Catholic church.'

Yeats' reference to Catholicism is interesting, for among the members of the Rhymer's Club, homosexuality went hand in hand with an almost morbid fascination with 'sin'. Wilde himself shared this fascination, although it was tempered by flippancy and irreverence. Among the young poets, the sense of sin was taken much more seriously. Perhaps because of this, a surprisingly high proportion became converts to Roman Catholicism – which places greater emphasis upon sin and upon its redemption than the Protestant churches.

Dowson, Beardsley, Johnson, Gray all became converts, as did Lord Alfred Douglas, many years later. Even Oscar Wilde was converted to Catholicism on his deathbed (claiming that he had been far too naughty before for the Church to accept him). Nearly all the members of the club died young or comparatively young, and many of the survivors including Symons, went mad.

To the majority of people, as the leader writers of the popular press declared, the whole thing had been

a bit of a hoot. For them, the significant event of the 'naughty '90s' – apart from the opportunity to assert their righteous indignation at the fate of Oscar Wilde – was the craze for the 'safety' bicycle (to which Thomas Hardy became devoted) and the 'new' woman seen pedalling through the countryside in her knickerbocker suit. The level of wit served up to the readers of newspapers was a far cry from the polished paradoxes of the decadents. 'The world is divided into two classes', declared one self-congratulatory wag, 'those who ride bicycles and those who don't.' This mania for cycling was behind the success of the musichall song *Daisy, Daisy, give me your answer do*, which competed in popularity with the nonsense chorus *Ta-ra-ra-boom-de-ay*, which, according to the social historian Holbrook Jackson, 'from 1892 to 1896 . . . affected the country like an epidemic'.

But if the decadents made little impression upon the populace, apart from their scandalous behaviour, Jackson discerned one important trait, which was perhaps common to both. Writing of the 1890s in 1913 he said, 'Life-tasting was the fashion, and the rising generation felt as though it were stepping out of the cages of convention and custom into a freedom full of tremendous possibilities'. A year later World War 1 broke out.

Aesthetic excess
(above) One of numerous popular songs which mocked the vogue for Aestheticism, My Aesthetic Love *was sung and sold 'with immense success'. The cover of the sheet music sums up the popular notion of self-conscious aesthetes – a lady, courted by a fop and cradling a sunflower, contemplates a lily in a room crammed with trendy paraphernalia. Blue china, oriental furniture and furnishings, peacocks' feathers and knick-knacks are prominent – all were available to the fashionable customers who flocked to Liberty's of London. Blue china was, claimed Wilde, something to be 'lived up to'. The craze was not to survive the death of Oscar Wilde or the end of the 19th century.*

SAMUEL BUTLER

✦ 1835-1902 ✦

Charles Gogin: Samuel Butler/National Portrait Gallery, London

Bitter resentment at an unhappy childhood set Butler
against all forms of dogmatism and authority; his witty
masterpiece is an autobiographical cry from the heart against
parents' inhumanity to children. Despite a personal gentleness
and wry sense of humour, his determination to challenge
Victorian hypocrisy and religion earned him hostile critics. He
shunned marriage, and lived as a semi-recluse, sustained by the
love of a few close friends.

Bachelor of Arts

An unorthodox and multi-talented figure, Butler – writer, painter and musician – delighted in controversy. But in spite of his clashes with the Establishment, he led the life of a quiet, eccentric bachelor.

A Victorian rebel, Samuel Butler would have been something of a rarity in any age. In addition to being a writer, he was an artist, photographer and musician, who seemed to enjoy nothing better than taking a recognized theory and showing the experts that they had got it wrong. Whether out of conviction, perversity or the sheer love of debating, Butler tackled religious, scientific and literary theories, repeatedly coming into conflict with the Establishment.

Butler was born in Langar, Nottinghamshire, on 4 December 1835, into a strict, upper-middle-class family. His father, Thomas, was a Reverend (and future Canon) of the Church of England, and his grandfather was a public (private) school headmaster and Bishop. Samuel's christening was

The Butler clan
The formidable Butler family (below) came of renowned stock. They were steeped in intractable, middle-class ethics and values which Samuel (far left) rejected. The substantial family home is sketched, left, in a letter by a cousin.

deferred until this eminent grandfather could perform it, and he later referred drily to the delay as a 'risky business', since 'all those months the devil had the run of me'. His relationship with his father was consistent from the start: 'He never liked me nor I him; from earliest recollections I can call to mind no time when I did not fear and dislike him . . .'

Butler's autobiographical novel *The Way of All Flesh* reveals the atmosphere and some precise details of his formative years. They were joyless and severe, as his heavy-handed, authoritarian and unsympathetic father tried to beat him into conformity. His earliest memories included Latin lessons at the age of four – 'my father thrashed it into me (I mean physically) day after day'. He also remembered a particularly momentous birthday: he had been given a jar of honey as a fourth birthday present, then 'My father came in, told us grandpapa was dead, and took away the honey, saying it would not be good for us.'

When Samuel was seven the gloom was relieved for a short while by a family trip to Italy, which yielded a life-long passion for that country. But his childhood was largely overshadowed by the Victorian public-school system, which he grew to know all too well at Shrewsbury School. Being a 'mere bag of bones' with 'no strength or stamina

'Family Prayers'
Butler painted the above picture in 1864. The figures are not true likenesses of his family, but the room is at Langar. It may have helped to exorcise unhappy memories of his repressively religious upbringing, for Butler referred to it as 'one of the very funniest things . . . I never finished it, but have kept it and hope it will not be destroyed after my death.' In pencil he wrote on the picture, 'if I had gone on doing things out of my own head instead of making copies I should have been all right' – a bitter post mortem on his other career as an artist.

The Master and Fellows, St. John's College, Cambridge

In a series of letters, Thomas Butler implored his son 'to settle on some profession' (by which he meant the Law, now that the Church had been dismissed). Samuel baited him, arguing that he wanted to make 'a fair survey of the prospect to see what may be most advantageous' (by which he meant a career as an artist, teacher, doctor, soldier or anything else his father did not want). He fully expected to be cut off from all financial support, but was not such a malcontent as to want to end all ties with home: 'I should be very sorry to think that any connection other than the money connection should cease.'

LIFE IN NEW ZEALAND

Eventually, aged 23, Butler settled on becoming a New Zealand sheep farmer, provoking his father's wrath – but not to the point at which his allowance would be stopped. Luckily for him, a last-minute shortage of passenger accommodation forced him to change ships – for the one on which he had intented to sail was lost with all hands. During the voyage he read copiously, learned to play the concertina, and organized a choir. On arrival he searched out 8000 acres of land and began life as a farmer.

New Zealand gave Samuel the chance to clarify his ideas and to spend time writing. He wrote in support of Darwin's evolutionary theories and in his letters home he recanted his religious faith entirely: 'A wider circle of idea has resulted from travel, and an entire uprooting of all past habits has been accompanied with a hardly less entire change of opinions'. He also had the satisfaction of making a profit from his farm, nearly doubling his £4400 which Thomas grudgingly sent him. Then in 1864, Butler met Charles Paine Pauli, a man who was to dominate the rest of his life.

whatsoever . . . useless and ill at ease with football' certainly did not help. According to his fictional hero Ernest in *The Way of All Flesh*, he survived by listening to his 'true self' and ignoring the brutality around him.

Butler's life changed when he went up to Cambridge aged 18. Here, at last, he was 'consciously and continuously happy'. He spent four years studying Classics, finally gaining a first class degree. He began writing and painting and discovered a passion for the music of Handel – 'his music has been the central fact of my life,' he wrote.

While at university, there were few opportunities for Butler to fall out with his father, but when he left Cambridge they did battle in earnest. It had long been assumed that, like his father and grandfather, Samuel would go into the Church. But he had other ideas. He felt no calling to live among the poor and benighted, dispensing goodness, charity and religious certitude. His objections to being ordained centred on a disbelief in infant baptism which he deduced had no effect on human behaviour: it could not turn a bad man into a good one.

Key Dates

1835 born Langar, Nottinghamshire

1854 enters Cambridge

1859 refuses to be ordained. Farms in New Zealand

1864 meets Pauli; returns to England

1867 meets Eliza Savage

1872 *Erewhon* published

1885 Eliza Savage dies

1886 father dies

1892-5 visits Italy, Greece, the Dardanelles

1902 dies in London

1903 *The Way of All Flesh* published

A student's vision

While still up at St John's, Cambridge, Butler painted the above study of the town. To him, university was joy unconfined – a place of learning as well as an escape from his family – and he was a brilliant scholar despite having many diverse interests.

Samuel Butler: Mr. Heatherley's Holiday. The Tate Gallery, London

nearly washed out as to have been with some difficulty deciphered'.

Back in London Butler lived 'almost the life of a recluse, seeing very few people.' But in 1867, he made perhaps his most important female friendship. Without the clever, witty Eliza Savage, it is doubtful whether he would have succeeded as a writer. She fired his enthusiasm to write his first novel *Erewhon*, and almost certainly encouraged him to tackle *The Way of All Flesh*, saying, 'it will be a perfect novel or as nearly so as may be'. The relationship could easily have led to marriage; Eliza wanted it, but Butler shunned matrimony.

Even if she had not been 'plain and lame and fat and short', as he crudely put it, Butler may still have preferred to keep his distance. For when he met Isabella Zanetti – the most beautiful woman he had ever seen – he also fled from her. Butler seems to have opted for an undemanding mistress: Lucie Dumas, a Frenchwoman. They met in London in 1872 and he visited her for the next 20 years. It was only after 15 years' acquaintance that he told her his name and address. In his correspondence, he always referred to Lucie as 'Madame'.

PATERNAL FURY

The publication of Butler's religious satire, *The Fair Haven* (1873), infuriated his father, and mortified his mother – something which Samuel was very unhappy to do. She was ill at the time, and told him that it 'tore open the wounds of the Redeemer'. She did not recover from her illness; and Thomas Butler blamed their son's book for her death, while Samuel acidly lamented, 'I had rather It had been my father.'

Pauli was everything Samuel was not – socially successful, athletic, suave and handsome. The 20-year-old would-be barrister realized he had made an instant conquest, and persuaded Butler to buy him a ticket back to England. Apparently the best of friends, they now took separate rooms at Clifford's Inn in London, with Butler anxious to finance Pauli's progress to the Bar. Increasingly, Pauli took more than he gave. If Butler could not afford to give him money, Pauli wept. If Butler tried to end the relationship, Pauli 'fell ill'.

Pauli did not hide his boredom at their dinner dates, and when he took new rooms he refused to give Butler his address. Yet he continued his emotional blackmail, regularly picking up a quarterly cheque from Butler long after his student days were over. When Butler wanted an opinion on what he had written and read it aloud to Pauli, he was 'the most freezing critic . . . in so far as he could be got to listen to a passage here and there'. Amazingly, the relationship lasted 30 years. Butler's feelings swung from adoration to wretchedness as he half realized that he was being exploited.

Butler recorded his experiences in New Zealand in *A First Year in the Canterbury Settlement*. The manuscript was lost overboard from a sinking ship and 'fished up from the Indian Ocean so

'Mr Heatherley's Holiday'

Butler numbered this painting among his best: it was exhibited in the Royal Academy, and depicts Thomas Heatherley, whose school of art Samuel attended. The school's students used to dress up the skeleton (kept for anatomical studies) and dance with it, so Mr Heatherley spent his vacations repairing the damage. The extraordinary debris accumulated by this cultured, eccentric man fills the background. Despite his teasing comments on Heatherley, Butler greatly admired him. Like Butler he was an artist, musician and scholar, and the two remained good friends.

BUTLER'S FARM

Butler called his New Zealand farmstead 'Mesopotamia' – the Greek for 'lying between two rivers'. Amid wild, uncharted grasslands, he played the piano, painted, read and engaged in bitter wrangles, by mail, with his father, seeking money for such urgent needs as a sheep dip. He recorded the first year in a factual book, and used the landscape in *Erewhon*.

The Master and Fellows. St. John's College, Cambridge

The Master and Fellows, St. John's College, Cambridge

The Master and Fellows, St. John's College, Cambridge

The Master and Fellows, St. John's College, Cambridge

A painful friendship
'Those years were very unhappy as well as very happy ones,' wrote Butler recalling Charles Paine Pauli (left), whom he loved, misguidedly, for 30 years with 'a white heat of devotion'.

Eliza Savage
(right) Witty, shrewd and cultured as she was, Eliza Savage could not capture Butler. After her death he wrote, 'She was too kind, wooed too persistently,/Wrote moving letters to me day by day;/ The more she wrote, the more unmoved was I,/The more she gave, the less could I repay.'

'My second country'
Butler fell in love with Italy as a boy and went back as often as he could, dedicating one book 'to her as a thank-offering for the happiness she has afforded me.' Below is his painting of Chiavenna, which he visited with Festing Jones.

Given such tensions, he did not stay long at Langar after the funeral, escaping to write what he intended to be an uncontroversial novel, 'pure and simple with little purpose'. He did note in passing, however, that he feared 'the cloven hoof will show itself again', and that is precisely what happened with *The Way of All Flesh*, a revenge on his father and on the Establishment which had made him so unhappy.

By his early 40s Samuel's life was stagnating. His painting was good enough to be included in several Royal Academy exhibitions, but his personal and financial life was less successful. His relationship with Pauli dragged on, and the investment of his capital in a Canadian patent steam-engine company was proving a mistake. Both he and Pauli had been made nominal directors in the Canada Tanning Extract Company, and whereas Pauli took no active role, Butler went out to Canada in 1874, 'fighting fraud of every kind' in an endeavour to save the company. Its eventual collapse reduced his capital to £2000, made him once more dependent on his father for an income, and left him feeling horribly guilty towards both Pauli and Pauli's brother whom he had involved in the investment.

Music and journeys to Italy sustained him until, in 1876, he made the second great friendship of his life, with his future biographer Henry Festing Jones, 'far and away the ablest man' he ever met.

When Samuel was 42 he gave up art ('my career . . . fizzled out') to concentrate on writing. He turned his attentions to science, tackling the major issue of the time – evolution. Although he had once been an enthusiastic believer in Darwin's theories, he now challenged the idea of natural selection from 'chance variations', preferring to take the view that species adapted by *active*

The Master and Fellows, St. John's College, Cambridge

learning, transmitted from one generation to the next by a kind of 'continuous memory'.

In 1885, Eliza Savage died. Butler wrote, 'It is out of the question I could ever replace her. I never knew any woman to approach her at once for brilliancy and goodness.' He planned an edition of the many letters which had passed between them, but abandoned the idea when he read those he sent, and was appalled at how 'meagre and egotistical they were'. Remorse increased after her

funeral. 'She haunts me, and always will haunt me because I never felt for her the love that if I had been a better man I would have felt.' In despair he abandoned the half-revised *The Way of All Flesh*.

The following year came another death – that of his father. There was to be no such remorse for him, just cynicism: 'One of the greatest feathers in his cap was . . . that he was *my* father.' According to Butler, 'the only person to whom he was ever really attached was the cat . . . me he simply detested'. It was not entirely true. Thomas had always wanted the best for his son and had always stood by him financially. In his will he left Samuel the sizeable income of £1200 a year. He also 'left' his son his clerk, Alfred Emery Cathie, who adopted the role of valet, arranging every little detail of Butler's life.

A QUIET DEMEANOUR

Although Butler's life might seem, in retrospect, to have been one long attempt to flout Victorian convention, no-one who met the man found him outrageous or anarchical. A contemporary description of him emphasizes his 'speaking softly and slowly, often with his head a little down' and having the manner of a 'kind old gentleman, prepared to be a little shocked by any disregard of proprieties.' Indeed, Butler balked at the idea of becoming a complete social outcast. 'I have the religious world bitterly hostile; the scientific and literary world are even more hostile than the religious; if to this hostility I am to add that of the respectable world, I may as well shut up shop at once.'

The mention of literary hostility refers to his shocking attempts in the 1880s to prove that *The Odyssey* was not written by Homer but by a Sicilian princess. To do this, he travelled exten-

Alfred Emery Cathie *(above) Despite the amused, paternal tone in which Butler mentions the uneducated simplicity of his 'clerk', Alfred was a devoted servant who for 15 years organized his master's everyday life. He put notes in Butler's pockets reminding him to have his beard trimmed, buy a new hat or go for a walk. Butler tried to teach him music and helped him save up to get married. There was always a message for Alfred in letters home from his travels abroad – from Sicily's classical ruins (below) for instance.*

sively in Sicily and Greece, and made similar journeys to the Dardanelles to check the 'archeological sites' of Homer's *Iliad*, although these did satisfy him as being correct.

His last major literary theory involved the re-ordering of Shakespeare's sonnets and a commentary which treats them as a series of love letters.

His argument mirrors remarkably his long, wretched affair with Pauli, for he condemns the recipient of the sonnets with such strength of feeling, saying he is 'vain, heartless, and I cannot think that he ever cared two straws for [someone] who no doubt bored him.'

Perhaps Butler was in part helped to come to

Belated affection
(above) 'Nothing but goodness and kindness ever came out of you . . . I feel as though I had lost an only son with no hope of another,' wrote Butler when his young friend, Hans Faesch, went home to Switzerland showing signs of grave illness.

Clifford's Inn
From the time he returned from New Zealand until his death, Butler lived in the same rather gloomy, spartan rooms, pictured left.

terms with his feelings towards Pauli by the last important friendship of his life, with a delightful young Swiss, Hans Faesch, whom he called his 'only son'. By contrast with Pauli, Faesch had such a gentle and friendly disposition that Butler named his placid, agreeable horse in the Dardanelles 'Hans' by way of compliment.

In 1897, Pauli died, and Butler was shocked to find that he had been swindling money out of two others as well as himself. He calculated that he had given Pauli £6500. Pauli had lived comfortably all along and left an estate of £9000. So this became a time for reflection for Butler, a time to 'edit his remains' (though he had no reason to think death particularly close). He wrote a detailed account of the Pauli affair, at least two sonnets to Eliza Savage and edited Henry Festing Jones's letters. Two more journeys to Italy followed, on the last of which he fell unexpectedly ill. He hurried home, was diagnosed to be suffering from pernicious anaemia, and appointed an executor to his £33,000 estate.

For the first time in his life, Samuel was gravely ill. Now pitiably 'shrunk, feeble and shockingly pale', he was removed from his old rooms to a nursing home. He died on 18 June 1902, aged 66, purportedly hoping that in the next world he would be among his favourites, Leonardo da Vinci, Homer, Shakespeare and Handel. Ever mindful of his abilities to provoke and annoy, he mischievously looked forward to catching sight of 'the shade of Charles Darwin [gliding] gloomily away when it sees me coming'.

Fact or Fiction

SELF-PORTRAIT

Ernest Pontifex is the young Samuel Butler. *The Way of All Flesh* is so heavily autobiographical that prison and marriage are virtually the only fictions in it. Butler quotes directly from letters, diaries and his music notebooks.

Inevitably, Ernest is musical, for Butler gave as much to music as to writing or art. He said of Handel, 'All day long – whether I am writing or painting or walking . . . I have his music in my head.' The portrait of Butler (right) reflects this. Butler was a competent musician, but perhaps the friend was correct who observed, 'He was too versatile a genius ever to be in the front rank of one particular line.'

HÆNDEL

All pictures from The Master and Fellows, St. John's College, Cambridge.

83

THE WAY OF ALL FLESH

Butler used his own life, word for word, deed by deed, for the story of Ernest Pontifex, a credulous but utterly credible hero who gradually learns the wicked ways of the world.

The novelist D. H. Lawrence described the 19th century as 'the age of the mealy-mouthed lie'. No 19th-century novel has dramatized what he meant more effectively than Samuel Butler's *The Way of All Flesh*. It is a crushing indictment of Victorian hypocrisy, where religious belief is convention more than conviction, marriage means prestige more than love and the family is not a safe haven but a prison. The special quality of Butler's masterpiece is undoubtedly attributable to the fact that the novel is in part autobiographical, while its charm derives from the wry good humour of the style.

Structurally, *The Way of All Flesh* takes the form of a *Bildungsroman* – that is, a novel about the formation of character from infancy to adulthood. It traces the spiritual education and development of Ernest Pontifex, as he gradually throws off the shackles of his 'virtuous' and 'respectable' family background.

GUIDE TO THE PLOT

The story is told by the hero's godfather, Edward Overton, a (barely tolerated) relation of the Pontifex family and an observer who does not significantly influence the action. It is Overton who establishes the novel's gently mocking tone of voice, and suggests to readers that we should share his affection for the poor, misguided hero of the piece. His dry, cynical wit goes with an ability to mask indignation behind a cloak of irony. For Overton is not an objective observer. He does not like Ernest's parents, and his status of confirmed bachelor makes him

Train up a child in the way he should go, and when he is old he will not depart from it.

My son, hear the instruction of thy father, and forsake not the law of thy mother.

Mary Evans Picture Library

the perfect vehicle for Butler's tart observations on marriage and the family.

It is some time before we are introduced to the hero himself, for Butler describes at great length Ernest's family predecessors. Ernest's ancestors certainly leave their mark on him. His musical and creative temperament he takes from his great-grandfather, John Overton, who is portrayed most sympathetically. But on a more negative note, Ernest has to overcome being grandson to George and son to the appalling Theobald and Christina.

At mother's knee
(left) Ernest Pontifex learns young that parents are not to be trusted. When Christina draws him close it is only to wheedle out some admission she may betray to her 'admirable' husband. And Ernest gets thrashed.

Musical salvation
(right) Music-loving Ernest is a 'throw-back' to his wholesome great-grandfather (inset), who built an organ for his local church.

A place in heaven?
(below) Ernest's father Theobald dislikes the duties of a vicar. He refuses to assure the dying of their place in Heaven – irritated by their pleas for reassurance.

Grandfather George Pontifex epitomizes the dangerous arrogance of the self-made man. He is self-opinionated, priggish and mean, with infinitely more fondness for money than mortals. Having decided that one of his sons should enter the Church (as a publisher of religious books, he thinks "this might tend to bring business"), George nominates the least impressive: Theobald. When Theobald makes his one and only gesture of defiance, George threatens to cut off his allowance, and rebellion is crushed. Theobald subsequently adopts the values of his father completely. It is the first hint

T. B. Kennington: Widowed and Fatherless (detail). Private Collection/Bridgeman Art Library

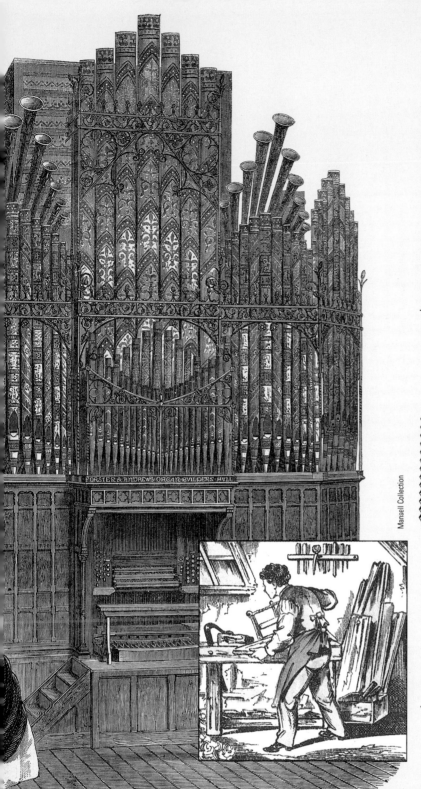

FORSTER & ANDREWS ORGAN BUILDERS HULL

Mansell Collection

Mary Evans Picture Library

The tuck shop
Well-meaning, guileless Ernest somehow succeeds in getting the tuck shop near school made out-of-bounds, and wrecks the minor economy founded on tuck-shop credit. It endears him neither to the boys, nor the headmaster, nor his father, nor the tuck shop proprietress (right).

James Collinson: The Bankrupt/Fine Art Photographic Library

> '*To parents ... I would say: Tell your children that they are very naughty ... Point to the young people of some acquaintances as models of perfection and impress your own children with a deep sense of their own inferiority ... This is called moral influence ...*'

Divine unrest
As divinity exams (below) approach and the prospect of being ordained comes close, Ernest suffers all the doubts his father felt before him. But Theobald threatens to cut his son off without a penny if he does not quash his pangs of conscience and take holy orders.

Alethea, who is impressed by a certain promise in his character. "He likes the best music and hates Dr Skinner. This is a very fair beginning." She confides to Overton that she plans to leave Ernest her money, but that it is only to be released to him on his 28th birthday.

Before then, Ernest has a lot to learn and the opportunity to make a great many mistakes. He leaps from one youthful conviction to the next – from high church to low church, from missionary zeal to rank atheism. He does nothing by halves. He is ordained a deacon and goes to live among the poor, only to be exploited and swindled by his spiritual comrade. In his innocent attempt to spread the word, he is arrested and subsequently imprisoned for

of the theme of parental 'persuasion'. In harness with Christina, "the most devotedly obsequious wife in all England", Theobald begins to practise his power on his children, notably Ernest.

Ernest grows up as a weak, frightened child, intimidated by his fearful father and baffled by his fluttery, treacherous mother. He is further demoralized when his education is entrusted to the headmaster of Roughborough Grammar School, Dr Skinner, who sees his task as the moulding of character and the championing of correct Latin pronunciation.

Ernest's only family friend is his aunt

Mary Evans Picture Library

Fate's pawn
When Ellen pawns Ernest's watch (left), his parents are keen to imagine the worst.

Bitter experience
More disillusion awaits in Ernest's first grimy London curacy (right).

a crime of which he is totally innocent.

Brain fever forces Ernest into a new awareness of his life and beliefs, with the result that he abruptly renounces Christianity and severs relations with his parents. He marries a former family servant, Ellen, but, to Overton's delight, Ellen proves to have 'a past'.

So, little by little, Ernest takes on the mantle of heroic failure, and begins to learn by his mistakes. But a change of fortune awaits him . . .

PERSONAL MUSINGS

In *The Way of All Flesh*, Butler mixes satire with his own brand of original philosophy – each the product of his hatred for contemporary domestic life. The Great Truth behind the book is that there are no Great Truths except that everyone has a duty to enjoy life and take everything with a pinch of salt – including literature. The book's fascination and appeal have little to do with its central character, and it does not satisfy a desire for pace and plot. For the story is interspersed with seemingly casual, but deceptively well-integrated, 'musings' – and it is here the book's strength lies. These musings are about family, religion, marriage and education, and give a fascinating insight into some of the philosophical controversies of the period. Butler's insights regarding the importance of the subconscious and of unresolved stresses within family life seem peculiarly modern; and his irreverent comments on matters religious must have scandalized

W. L. Wyllie; London From the Monument/Fine Art Photographic Library

his dogmatically pious contemporaries.

The novel contains some superb comic set-pieces: Ernest's attempt at saving a 'prostitute'; George Pontifex's cultural tour of Italy; the card game in which Christina wins her chance to set her cap at Theobald. The coach journey after their wedding is a humorous *tour de force* in which the internal monologues of the craven Theobald are set alongside those of Christina, who looks "a little older than she quite liked to look as a bride who had been married that morning".

For all his exasperation at her subservience and day-dreaming, Butler remains torn between amusement and anger at Christina. "If it were not such an awful thing to say of anyone," Overton

---

In the Background

BURLESQUE THEATRE

Edward Overton, the narrator, writes for burlesque theatre. Originally burlesque was satirical drama 'spoofing' topical celebrities or literary works. After a sophisticated 18th-century heyday, the term 'burlesque' broadened to include general comedy. The most famous writer of the day was H. J. Byron with plays such as *The Corsican Brothers* (above).

Mansell Collection

'... a scared, insulted girl, flushed and trembling, was seen hurrying from Mrs Jupp's ... in another ten minutes two policemen were seen also coming out of Mrs Jupp's, between whom there shambled rather than walked our unhappy friend Ernest, with staring eyes, ghastly pale, and with despair branded upon every line of his face.'

Unwanted advances
What better place to start his evangelical work than in his own boarding house? But Ernest's well-intentioned advances to a respectable seamstress (above) land him in gaol (right) where the shame caused by his downfall all but kills him.

observes, "I should say that she meant well." By contrast, the satirical attacks which Butler directs at Theobald barely disguise the author's angry and painful feelings towards his own father. The scene where Theobald beats the boy for pronouncing the word 'come' as 'tum' is utterly chilling. The author's 'humour' is barbed and bitter even when he describes Theobald's response to his wife's death:
"*She has been the comfort and mainstay of my life for more than thirty years,*" *said Theobald as soon as all was over,* "*but one could not wish it prolonged,*" *and he buried his face in his handkerchief to conceal his want of emotion.*

HYPOCRISY EXPOSED
The abiding theme of the novel is the misery and hypocrisy of Victorian life, ruled as it was by convention. Butler exposes a devastating contrast between the respectable façade of Victorian family life and the callousness and cruelty it could conceal. Theobald and Christina are perceived by their neighbours as models of Victorian parenthood, but their moral bullying and brutality eventually drive their son to rebellion and alienation. Yet they neither suffer for their cruelty nor are they even made to recognize it – and very few others seem to see through them.

When Theobald dies, Ernest is engulfed by letters of condolence. And when Ernest – whose only sin is innocence in a naughty world – is sentenced to imprisonment, the magistrate's speech about the 'advantages' of Ernest's upbringing is all too horribly credible. With portraits of hyprocrites like this, arrogantly impervious to their own ignorance, Butler piles up instances of the humbug of his age. Against it, he counsels distrust, scepticism and contempt, particularly towards all those authoritarian figures whom society and tradition teach us to revere – parents, clergymen, teachers, magistrates.

The Way of All Flesh remains one of fiction's best planted bombs under the myth of Victorian virtue and domestic peace. At the time of its publication (the year after Butler's death), it came as a luxurious relief to those cramped by the moral and emotional straight-jacket of the previous era. It was championed by many artists of the time. George Bernard Shaw loved its 'extraordinarily fresh, free and future-piercing suggestions'. E. M. Forster said that 'it taught me how to look at money'. Virginia Woolf saw it as one of those novels that change man's idea of himself and can simultaneously change attitudes to religion, conduct, politics and literature. *The Way of All Flesh* might not be one of the most perfectly constructed novels, but it is among the most influential, unforgettable and amazingly un-Victorian works of Victorian fiction.

Breaking the mould
Ernest has his children raised in rural simplicity (below), free of "the misery of false expectations" – and very happy.

CHARACTERS IN FOCUS

The characters in *The Way of All Flesh* are presented to us by the narrator, Overton, whose ironical cast of mind and particular prejudices and preferences are central to the novel's style and tone. Essentially, Overton speaks with Butler's own voice. The author is also fond of revealing characters by quoting their letters in which they inadvertently condemn themselves.

Christina, the ruthless, dreamer (above), entertains great ambitions for her children, hoping their lives will reflect well on her. Convinced of her own piety and her family's adoration, she is ignorant of their true feelings.

WHO'S WHO

Edward Overton The narrator: a cynical, irreverent, confirmed bachelor.

Ernest Pontifex The guileless hero attempting to find his way in the world and keep a good conscience.

Theobald Pontifex Rector of Battersby-on-the-Hill; Ernest's tyrannical father, long since cowed and moulded by his own, equally tyrannical father.

Christina Pontifex Ernest's sentimental but heartless and egocentric mother.

George Pontifex Theobald's middle-class father who organizes the fates of his children according to market forces.

John Pontifex Ernest's great-grandfather; a carpenter and musician, he was the sound rootstock of the family.

Alethea Ernest's rebellious aunt and benefactress and Overton's sweetheart.

Dr Skinner Headmaster of Roughborough Grammar School – a one-time academic genius, but inane and unimaginative.

Ellen Servant at the Rectory; later Ernest's wife.

Charlotte Ernest's sister. "When I have a bad dream, I dream that I have got to stay with Charlotte", he says.

Pryer A persuasive, articulate, untrustworthy radical under whose influence Ernest falls.

Edward Overton (left), though he is Ernest's godfather, has little contact with him until his beloved Alethea takes Ernest under her wing. Then Overton is obliged to watch over the boy while holding his legacy in trust. Edward is a gently subversive influence, but allows Ernest to make his own mistakes and discoveries without intervening. He maintains a detached, wry, ironical view of life, but a paternal fondness comes across which lends him much humanity. One of his 'professions' is as a playwright, but "If I was a light of literature, it was of the very lightest kind."

National Gallery of Scotland, Edinburgh/Bridgeman Art Library

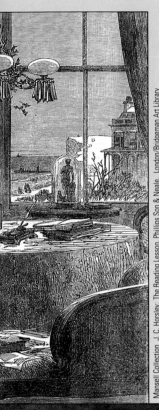

"It might have been better if Theobald [left] in his younger days had kicked more against his father: the fact that he had not done so encouraged him to expect the most implicit obedience from his own children." Intolerant and full of spleen, Theobald is irritated by his son from the very day of his birth. He sets himself the task, which he perceives as his Christian duty, of curbing the boy's will. *"He began to whip him two days after he had begun to teach him."*

Mansell Collection. J. C. Horsley: The Reading Lesson. Phillips Son & Neale, London/Bridgeman Art Library

City of Manchester Art Galleries

Ernest (left) finds that "growing is . . . hard work – harder than any but a growing boy can understand . . . You are surrounded on every side by lies." Thus he struggles towards the light of understanding, lurching from one extreme conviction to another until he finds *"that the principal business of life is to enjoy it."*

Witty and generous, Alethea Pontifex (below) *"was determined, so she said, to make the rest of her life as happy as she could."* Despite *"the most perfect sympathy"* between her and Overton, they never marry.

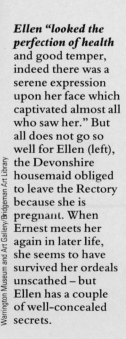

Warrington Museum and Art Gallery/Bridgeman Art Library

Ellen "looked the perfection of health and good temper, indeed there was a serene expression upon her face which captivated almost all who saw her." But all does not go so well for Ellen (left), the Devonshire housemaid obliged to leave the Rectory because she is pregnant. When Ernest meets her again in later life, she seems to have survived her ordeals unscathed – but Ellen has a couple of well-concealed secrets.

Frith: Lady with Parasol. Roy Miles Fine Paintings, London/Bridgeman Art Library

DEVIL'S ADVOCATE

It was not sheer perversity which made Butler take the opposing view on so many subjects: he wrote from the heart. But he undoubtedly loved a good argument.

'I am the *enfant terrible* of literature and science. If I cannot, and I know I cannot, get the literary and scientific big-wigs to give me a shilling, I can, and I know I can, heave bricks into the middle of them.'

This entry in one of Butler's notebooks summarizes his role in late Victorian England, and hints at the price he paid for it in critical neglect and commercial failure. He began his literary career with a relative success in *Erewhon* (1872), a fantasy social satire which actually showed a small profit. The book appeared anonymously – which, according to Butler, made the critics respectful in case it was written by somebody 'important'. Indeed, *Erewhon* was widely believed to be the work of the aristocrat novelist, Lord Lytton. Once the truth was known, sales fell from 50 a week to two or three.

Butler had to pay to have his books published, even *Erewhon*, and all his

The Master and Fellows, St. John's College, Cambridge

subsequent ones lost money. Most sold no more than a few hundred copies, and at the end of his life Butler reckoned that he was more than £900 out of pocket in his dealings with publishers. Although he pretended not to care, he gave himself away from time to time. For example, in a letter to his sister, commenting on the fortunes made by Thomas Carlyle and Herbert Spencer, he argued that 'their careers tend to show that after a time persistent writing does force its way. I never was so much abused before as now . . . I cannot but think that there will be a turn in the tide ere long.'

But the tide never turned, and even the abuse was not sustained enough to make Butler a public figure. In 1886, looking over the obituaries of Canon Butler, he noted bitterly to his brother that 'It was nowhere said that he was the father of the present writer, and this shewed me (but I wanted no shewing) how very little my books are known.'

The most important reason for Butler's lack of success was probably that he belonged to no definable literary or political group, and wrote in such a way as to offend those who did. *The Fair Haven*,

Mary Evans Picture Library

Erstwhile hero
Although he once defended Charles Darwin against those who lampooned him (left), Butler crossed him by publicly favouring earlier evolutionary theories.

A writer's room
Butler's sitting-room at Clifford's Inn (right) was painted a dirty white, and hung with his own sketches and photographs of Italian pictures. It also contained his piano. Next door was his painting room.

No regrets
Butler (left) attributed his character to his icy, painful upbringing. In his view, his talent and abilities were the tools of survival he had used to triumph in adversity. "If I had to be born again I would be born . . . of the same father and mother as before, and I would not alter anything that has ever happened to me."

published the year after *Erewhon*, was doubly shocking. It denied the reality of the Resurrection and other Biblical miracles while appearing to defend and affirm them – and achieved this so cleverly that a number of unsuspecting clergymen actually praised the book from the pulpit. After this, reviewers were probably wary of being hoaxed by Butler.

Butler's other subjects were just as badly chosen from a commercial point of view. While religiously orthodox people were furiously denouncing the evolutionary theories of Charles Darwin, Butler put forward an alternative theory that displeased both the pro- and anti-Darwinists. He rejected the notion of Divine Creation, not for Darwin's theory of natural selection but the idea of 'creative evolution'. And at a time when the Oscar Wilde scandal was still fresh in the public mind he published *Shakespeare's Sonnets, Reconsidered* (1899), touching on the passionate relationship between the poet and a certain Mr W. H., to whom the sonnets were dedicated. Added to this, during a period when the Classics were solemnly venerated and the sexes knew

The Master and Fellows, St. John's College, Cambridge

their places, Butler translated the *Iliad* and the *Odyssey* into a vigorously colloquial and irreverent modern prose, and argued forcefully that the *Odyssey* must have been written by a woman. Here, as elsewhere, his championship of obscure and unpopular causes sometimes smacks of sheer contrariness.

As a member of the leisured class – however worried he may sometimes have been about his financial situation – Butler could well afford to indulge his interests. There was certainly something of the dilettante in a man who could work at painting and composing music, as well as writing critical works on a disconcerting variety of topics. Yet Butler might have achieved less if he had been forced to earn a living by his pen.

More than most writers, Butler relied on inspiration. He told his friend Miss Savage that he could write on a subject only 'because I am bursting with it'. And after the publication of *The Fair Haven*, when she urged him to write a novel, he answered 'I do not know what I shall write next. I do not want to write anything in particular and shall paint until an idea strikes me which I must work out or die, like *The Fair Haven*. I shall do nothing well unless *con amore* [with love], and under divine inspiration.' Or, as he advised himself more pithily in his notebooks, 'Only do that which insists upon being done and runs right up against you,

Blasphemous doubt
In The Fair Haven *Butler argues, albeit in the guise of an ardent believer, that Christ did not die on the Cross (left) and that there was no miraculous Resurrection.*

Face of the past
Butler used an Etruscan painting (right) seen in Cortona, Italy, as the frontispiece of his book The Authoress of the Odyssey. *It clearly matches his concept of the Sicilian princess he claimed had written the revered classic.*

Rubens: Descent from the Cross. Courtauld Institute, London/Fotomas

Museo dell' Accademia Etrusca di Cortina./Scala

hitting you in the eye until you do it.'

However, Butler was well prepared to catch inspiration on the wing. He carried a small pad in his waistcoat pocket, and made frequent notes of ideas, conversations and happenings that caught his attention. These jottings, written out and expanded at home, accumulated rapidly; and during the last ten years of his life Butler made it a rule to spend an hour a day pruning, editing and indexing them. At his death he left five bound volumes, each consisting of 225 pages of closely written sermon paper; and in selected

Student home
As a student at St John's College, Cambridge, Butler lived in rooms at New Court (right). The college now possesses many of his papers and paintings, including the picture and map below.

"Alps and Sanctuaries"
This travel book, with many philosophical and comic asides, met mostly with 'sneering reviews'. Miss Savage had foreseen low sales: 'the book is not exactly adapted for a school prize, which is a pity.' Butler illustrated the work himself with such pictures as the one above.

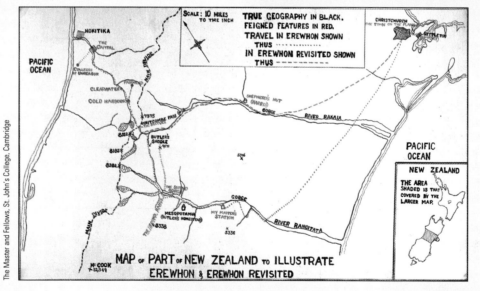

MAP OF PART OF NEW ZEALAND TO ILLUSTRATE EREWHON & EREWHON REVISITED

Mapping Erewhon
A fascinating map survives (left) showing precisely the landscape Butler had in mind as he wrote Erewhon *and just how far he departed from fact. His true-life, arduous, anxious search for a suitable piece of land to farm, is recorded in the opening chapters of the book, as the hero seeks out pastureland of his own.*

form, these published *Notebooks* (1912) are among his most fascinating works, crowded with lively arguments, aphorisms and paradoxes.

In the notebooks Butler gives a trenchant account of his approach to writing. Apart from asserting that a writer should only set to work when a subject 'insists upon being done', Butler announces that the writing itself should never be studied. He blames art schools for his 'years of vague aspiration and despair', claiming with some justice that he ended a worse painter than he started out. Fortunately

(according to Butler) there was no-one to teach him writing; so he learned as he went along. Others, he asserts, should do likewise: 'Don't learn to do, but learn in doing. Let not your falls be on prepared ground, but let them be bona fide falls in the rough and tumble of the world . . . Act more and rehearse less.'

Butler's views on style are equally uncompromising: the writer must think of the reader, not of himself. Although many of Butler's well-known contemporaries worked hard to forge a graceful, 'individual' manner, 'I never knew a

writer yet who took the smallest pains with his style and was at the same time readable . . . A man may, and ought to, take a great deal of pains to write clearly, tersely and euphoniously: he will write many a sentence three or four times over . . . he will be at great pains to see that he does not repeat himself, to arrange his matter in the way that shall best enable the reader to master it . . . but in each case he will be thinking not of his own style but of his reader's convenience'. His own 'style', Butler declared, was 'just common, simple straightforwardness'.

paradoxes that he himself might have relished. He was not by instinct a novelist, yet he is remembered above all for his novel, *The Way of All Flesh*. It is an outspoken work by a writer who challenged the Victorian Establishment on many issues; but he did not dare (or was too considerate) to publish it during his lifetime. And, although his undoubted masterpiece, it was the only one of his books of whose value Butler was not entirely certain. Urged on by Miss Savage, he intermittently wrote and rewrote the novel for 12 years. The last part, in his view, needed considerable revision, but when Miss Savage died in 1885 he put the manuscript away and never looked at it again. Butler certainly hoped that posterity would grant him the recognition that his contemporaries withheld, but there is no evidence that he believed *The Way of All Flesh* to be his masterpiece.

POSTHUMOUS FAME

Butler's last book, *Erewhon Revisited*, was a satire on religion, potent enough to frighten off his usual publisher, Longmans. He was persuaded to consult the Irish playwright George Bernard Shaw, who introduced Butler to his own publisher, Grant Richards. The outcome was that for the first time – not long before Butler's death – the publisher, rather than Butler himself, financed the production and distribution of one of his books.

To Shaw, Butler was 'in his own department the greatest English writer of the latter half of the 19th century'. During the early 1900s Shaw was becoming a world-famous figure, and his energetic advocacy transformed Butler's reputation. The posthumously published *The Way of All Flesh* was widely read, and in the 1920s – when World War I had discredited the old English certainties – the tide turned and the novel assumed its present status as an undisputed classic.

As a writer, Butler's humour is similarly uncontrived, owing relatively little to amusing situations or phraseology: Butler is funny because he is free from common prejudices and views things from unusual angles. Among his many entertaining and unexpected sayings are such gems as 'To put one's trust in God is only a longer way of saying that one will chance it' and 'In matrimony, to hesitate is sometimes to be saved'.

Butler's reputation involves a set of

Biographies
Henry Festing Jones (seen left with Butler) was his friend, executor and biographer. Butler himself spent years on a biography of his grandfather (below).

The Master and Fellows, St. John's College, Cambridge. Inset London Library

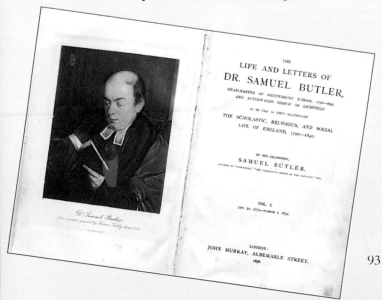

THE
LIFE AND LETTERS OF
DR. SAMUEL BUTLER,
HEAD-MASTER OF SHREWSBURY SCHOOL, 1798–1836,
AND AFTERWARDS BISHOP OF LICHFIELD

IN SO FAR AS THEY ILLUSTRATE
THE SCHOLASTIC, RELIGIOUS, AND SOCIAL
LIFE OF ENGLAND, 1790–1840.

BY HIS GRANDSON,
SAMUEL BUTLER,
AUTHOR OF "EREWHON," "THE FAIR HAVEN OF THE NATION," ETC.

VOL. I.

JAN. 30, 1774—MARCH 1, 1831.

LONDON:
JOHN MURRAY, ALBEMARLE STREET.
1896.

'I have never written on any subject unless I believed that the authorities on it were hopelessly wrong.' Samuel Butler believed they were wrong about a great many things, and proceeded to set them right – as he saw it – in his own forthright, entertaining style.

He was in his late thirties, however, before his first work of substance, the paradoxical 'utopian' *Erewhon*, was published in 1872. It was followed by *The Fair Haven* (1873), an ironic pseudo-defence of the miraculous element in Christianity. Then *Life and Habit* (1878) began Butler's long involvement in the controversies over the theory of evolution, in which he took up a position that offended both the orthodox religious and the orthodox scientific communities. Two books of travel and art criticism bear witness to his deep love of Italy. The meaning of Shakespeare's sonnets and the authorship of Homer's *Odyssey* were among Butler's later preoccupations, and at the end of his life he brought his work full circle with *Erewhon Revisited* (1901).

EREWHON
◆ 1872 ◆

Erewhon, or, Over the Range (right and below) is a delightful mixture of satire and fantasy. It is supposedly written by a man who has gone out to an unnamed colony, where he works for a sheep-farmer. Crossing a mountain range into unexplored territory, he discovers Erewhon ('Nowhere' backwards – if, like Butler, you count *wh* as a single letter). The Erewhonians are a people of remarkable physical beauty, but their customs and ideas bewilder the narrator. He is kept in prison while he learns the Erewhonian language, intimately assisted by the jailer's beautiful daughter, Yram. Erewhon, it turns out, is a country where crime is treated as a form of illness, whereas illness, poverty and bad luck are punished as criminal activities. The narrator eventually manages to escape from Erewhon by balloon – a feat that has startling consequences for the Erewhonians.

Private Collection/Bridgeman Art Library

EREWHON REVISITED
◆ 1901 ◆

This sequel to **Erewhon** describes the further adventures of its narrator, whose name – Higgs – is given in this book for the first time. The story is told by the son of Higgs and Arowhena. Twenty years after his escape, Higgs revisits Erewhon in disguise and discovers that there have been extraordinary changes. His balloon flight has been interpreted as an ascent to heaven, and as 'the Sunchild' he is now the centre of a religious cult. His sayings, real and invented, have become Holy Writ, and like other religions Sunchildism has split into competing schools and sects. Respectable orthodoxy is represented by two outright frauds, Hanky and Panky, Professors of Worldly and Unworldly Wisdom. Higgs discovers that he has a son, George, the offspring of his brief relationship with Yram. To win George's love he declares his true identity. He comes close to being burned alive as a heretic, but George and Yram pass him off as a harmless lunatic. Half deranged by his experiences, he returns to England and dies, unaware that Anglo-Erewhonian contacts are far from at an end.

The Museum of London

Private Collection/Bridgeman Art Library

F. R. Pickersgill: Mother and Child with Poppy, Roy Miles Gallery, London/Bridgeman Art Library

LIFE AND HABIT
◆ 1878 ◆

The relationship of mother and child (left) is one of the themes explored in this the first of Butler's four books on Evolution, which still reads freshly enough to have merited recent republication. Butler wrote in reaction against Charles Darwin's theory of natural selection – that organisms evolve as a result of chance modifications, selected or eliminated according to 'the survival of the fittest'. Darwin, said Butler, 'banished Mind from the universe', of which he had 'a purely automatic conception . . . as of something that will work if a penny is dropped into a box'.

Butler's version of the evolutionary process was influenced by earlier writers such as the French biologist Lamarck, viewing changes in an organism as the result of its own will and effort; essentially, all its characteristics were created by the same kind of process as that by which an athlete intentionally builds up muscles or particular skills. This theory committed Butler to a belief that characteristics acquired during the parents' lifetime could be transmitted to the offspring.

Butler elaborated several fascinating ideas (such as the identification between parent and child before birth, and the existence of a common memory across the generations) that influenced later biologists and psychologists.

THE AUTHORESS OF THE ODYSSEY
◆ 1897 ◆

Butler was fascinated by the story of Ulysses (**or Odysseus**) (right), here shown in one of the most famous scenes from his legend. To avoid the enchantment of the Sirens, who lured sailors to their deaths with the sweetness of their songs, he ordered his crew to stop up their ears with wax. Ulysses wanted to hear their singing, however, so he had himself tied to the ship's mast and thus could not be lured to his doom however seductive their voices. This story is told in the *Odyssey* by the Greek poet Homer – one of the masterpieces of world literature. Butler was an accomplished classical scholar, but his ideas on Homer were extremely unconventional. In the 1890s he devoted much of his time to research on the poem, writing articles about it in both English and Italian and also lecturing on the subject. He summed up his thoughts in this book, in which he maintained that the *Odyssey* was written in Sicily and by a woman. A few people praised Butler's freshness and 'common sense' approach, but in general his book was badly received by scholars and public alike. Two years after publication it had sold only 165 copies and Butler made a loss of over £80 on it. Butler also made prose translations of the *Odyssey* (1900) and of Homer's other great poem, the *Iliad* (1898).

Herbert Draper: Ulysses and the Sirens. Ferens Art Gallery, Hull/Bridgeman Art Library

Fallen Angels

**Victorian morality was rife with hypocrisy – sexual codes were
entirely different for men and women, and it was often the
innocent who paid 'the price of sin'.**

To a generation brought up on sexual liberation and women's rights, the Victorian age presents astonishing contradictions in attitude. For this society, which purported to live by a rigid moral code, and upheld the sanctity of marriage, supported a larger number of prostitutes than at any time before or since.

It was just such hypocrisy that Butler attacked in *The Way of All Flesh*. For middle-class men and women of the Victorian era, sexual repression was the norm within marriage, and resulted in the grossest of double standards. Women were divided into two classes: those to whom sex was an unmentionable indelicacy and those who satisfied men's 'needs'. The extraordinary inconsistencies in the Victorian outlook were magnified as the century progressed, as middle-class attitudes increasingly dominated society.

THE IDEAL OF MARRIAGE

Middle-class morality dictated that sexual intercourse was a dark and evil thing. This notion was ingrained from birth and fuelled by medical and religious opinion. By contrast, marriage was a sacred institution which, although it necessitated the begetting of children, should be based on a pure and noble love.

Marriage was every young woman's goal. It conferred respectability, financial security and status, coupled with the satisfaction of rearing children. Romantic love, pure and unsullied (real or imagined), was eagerly anticipated. (The reality was often different, of course, and divorce extremely difficult, carrying with it a social stigma.) Most women entered marriage ignorant of the realities of sexual intercourse. For some, their wedding night was an experience little short of rape. For others, the intimacy of sex may not have been as traumatic or as disagreeable as they had been led to expect. But pleasure itself could bring guilt, for sex within marriage was considered neither genteel nor moral except for the purpose of conceiving children.

Medical opinion, underlining these attitudes, recommended marital sex no more than once a month, and stated that respectable women had no sexual desire. One distinguished writer, Dr William Acton, maintained: '. . . the majority of women (happily for them) are not very much troubled with sexual feeling of any kind. What

Adultery
The painting below is the first of three (see p. 98) which depict the dissolution of a family. Here the wife's infidelities have just been discovered via an incriminating letter. Her husband grinds her lover's portrait underfoot while the children's house of cards collapses – a darkly symbolic omen.

A royal wedding
Britain's royal family exemplified the double standards inherent in Victorian society. The Prince of Wales' marriage to Alexandra of Denmark (right) was a splendid state occasion. But Edward clearly considered himself above the marriage vows and had a succession of notorious liaisons.

Mary Evans Picture Library

Lily Langtry
Noted for her beauty, the actress Lily (or Lillie) Langtry was Edward the Prince of Wales' most celebrated mistress. Born Emily Charlotte le Breton in 1852, Lily was twice married and had numerous other lovers, including the Crown prince Rudolf of Austria and King Leopold II of Belgium.

or at least, low and vulgar women. [But] No nervous or feeble young man need be deterred from marriage by an exaggerated notion of the duties required of him. The married woman has no notion to be treated on the footing of a mistress.'

In these few words, Acton assembled all the unhealthy assumptions governing Victorian life: that both men and women feared marriage; that most Victorian men were presumed to have had a sexually demonstrative prostitute or mistress prior to marriage; and that the respectable wife took no interest or delight in sex. Yet for the many high-minded men who did succeed in stifling or sublimating their sexual desires before the wedding night, marriage could be as traumatic as for their wives.

Such men, before and after marriage, found compensation for their unsatisfied or baffling sexuality in platonic friendships with other men, or even in religion or zealous good works. And for others, unable or unwilling to visit prostitutes, there was a plentiful supply of pornography, catering for all tastes.

Private Collection/Bridgeman Art Library

men are habitually, women are only exceptionally . . . The best mothers, wives and managers of households know little of sexual indulgences. Love of home, children and domestic duties are the only passions they feel.'

Very many women would have agreed with him, for consciously or unconsciously their sexual feelings were repressed. This repression may have given rise to the many 'nervous' disorders to which Victorian women were prone. One practical disincentive to sex, however, must have been the fear of pregnancy at a time when childbirth was often fatal, and when repeated pregnancies sapped a woman's health and energy.

Men's sexual desires were acknowledged, but it was their moral duty to stifle them. Marriage to a virtuous woman was the one hope of channelling – and eventually dampening – sexual desire. Often men had such an ambivalent attitude to sex that they positively feared marriage. Dr Acton had this advice for them: 'Many men, and particularly young men, form their ideas of women's feelings from what they notice early in life among loose,

PRIVILEGED PROMISCUITY

The morality which came to obsess the middle class did not really extend to either the upper or working classes. Their lives were as 'free' as they had ever been. The poor frequently stopped short of marriage; and the aristocracy modified its promiscuous behaviour only when scandal threatened. Queen Victoria was refreshingly direct about the pleasures of married life with her beloved Albert, and later was remarkably under-

Idealized womanhood
Some men knew about women's bodies only from art. The writer John Ruskin was reputedly appalled to discover his wife had pubic hair.

Augustus Egg: The Adulteress and her Fate I. The Tate Gallery, London

Alexandre Cabanel: Birth of Venus, Louvre, Paris/Lauros-Giraudon/Bridgeman Art Library

calculated that £8,000,000 was being spent on prostitution each year. The top price paid to a fairly high-class prostitute was one or two pounds, while a few pence bought the pathetic, disease-ridden creatures from the slums of London's East End.

Henry Mayhew, famous for his masterly study *London Labour and the London Poor* (1851–62), divided prostitutes into groups of descending order: kept mistresses and 'prima donnas'; independent women and lodging-house (brothel) women supervised by a madam; low lodging women; sailors' and soldiers' women; park women (dossers); and thieves' women.

The high-class kept women and 'prima donnas' lived a life that was envied not only by their fellow prostitutes but also, perhaps, by the respectable Victorian wife. They lived in fashionable lodgings, were elegantly and expensively dressed, and were seen, with their aristocratic admirers, horse-riding in Hyde Park. Their social status was such that they suffered little from scandal-mongering or ostracism.

ROYAL MISTRESSES

Their attractions often included charm and wit was well as beauty, and they lived in fine style. Catherine Walters (Skittles) and Lily Langtry, both of them friends of the Prince of Wales, were among the most famous. They were not necessarily even single women: the 'Jersey Lily' was married when the Prince met her, and the onus was on her husband to turn a blind eye in the interest of his betters. Harriet Wilson was a courtesan who, in later life when down on her luck, threatened the Duke of Wellington with blackmail – but failed. 'Publish and be damned', he replied when she offered to expunge him from her memoirs for a 'consideration'.

While not attaining this level of fame or infamy, a successful young prostitute could aspire to marriage with one of her clients – a young shopkeeper, say, or a clerk who was not averse to a bride with a few savings. Occasionally they married men of some standing. One fortunate prostitute married a wealthy Norfolk landowner who settled a substantial income on her. His outraged relatives sought a court order declaring him insane, but failed. (He was admittedly a little eccentric and liked to dress up as a minor railway official.) Others, not so lucky as to achieve marriage, were set up in some small suburban house, usually by a member of the professional classes, who visited them regularly while maintaining a wife and children elsewhere.

By far the largest group of prostitutes were the part-timers and street-walkers in the industrial cities, many of whom were driven to prostitution by sheer poverty. However harsh life was in rural areas, the scope for, and rewards of, commercial sex were limited. In the cities, however, there was ample opportunity.

Mayhew describes the plight of a young woman who was a shirt-maker with a small child. She

standing about the sexual scandals in which the Prince of Wales was involved. But a handful of intellectuals, such as Samuel Butler, detected and scorned the double standards emerging among their own (middle) class.

There are no reliable statistics, but it has been estimated that in the latter half of the 19th century there were 120,000 prostitutes in London alone. It is unclear whether this includes the vast majority of 'irregulars' (prostitutes who worked only when times were hard), child prostitutes or the many thousands of 'kept' women. It has also been

A moral tale
Continuing the story of the adulterous wife, we are shown her daughters some years later, longing for maternal love (top). Their mother (above) is in more desperate straits, alone and sleeping rough, clutching the child born of her ill-starred, long past affair.

The Adulteress and her Fate II and III. The Tate Gallery, London

earned two-and-a-half pennies for each shirt – which did not even pay for a roof over her head. Forced into prostitution, she tried, from time to time, to give it up, for the sake of the child. But on one occasion, when she was homeless, her little boy's legs froze to her sides as she carried him. Although she and the boy were saved by an act of kindness, she went back to prostitution subsequently, as the only means of survival. There were many thousands of young women in a similar position, who would have liked to live decently if they had had a choice. Seamstresses, servant girls (dollymops) and milliners' assistants were among those who fell into this poverty trap.

The lives of brothel prostitutes varied according to the class of brothel which housed them. These women at least had a roof over their heads, and some had their food and clothing provided. But a large portion of their earnings was taken by their pimp or madam.

The prostitutes who frequented the dockland slums in London and other ports were in a different class altogether. On Mayhew's list these were the 'lowest of the low'. At any one time, there were thousands of sailors of all nationalities at loose in the dock areas, who had money to spend on drink and sex. Conditions in these areas were indescribably foul. The squat houses and narrow streets were filled with beggars and thieves as well as whores, living many to a room in crumbling and squalid lodging houses.

Here most of the prostitutes were alcoholic or

Jan Van Beers: The Courtesan. Gavin Graham Gallery/Bridgeman Art Library

Mansell Collection

THE GREAT SOCIAL EVIL.

TIME:—Midnight. A Sketch not a Hundred Miles from the Haymarket.

Bella. "AH! FANNY! HOW LONG HAVE YOU BEEN *GAY?*"

Successful sinner
(above) A high-class prostitute or kept woman could enjoy a life of luxury, pampered and clad in extraordinary finery.

A fallen woman
(left) A poorly dressed woman asks a much smarter companion how long she has been on the game ('gay' was a euphemism for 'immoral'). The scene is London's Haymarket, renowned for its streetwalkers and known at the time as 'Hell Corner'.

Backstage encounters
(right) For women who wanted to climb the social ladder, the stage offered a potential first rung. Those endowed with sufficient charms might discover the key to a better future backstage.

Mansell Collection

the plight of the 'fallen woman'. Their motives and mentalities varied. For some there may have been a subconscious sexual thrill to be had from their 'good works'. William Gladstone, the Prime Minister, is well known for his (no doubt) chivalrous attempts to reclaim prostitutes, but was attacked for it by one of his parliamentary colleagues: 'Gladstone manages to combine his missionary meddling with keen appreciation of a pretty face. He has never been known to rescue any of our East End whores, nor for that matter is it easy to contemplate him rescuing an ugly woman.'

IMPASSIONED CRUSADERS

Writers such as Thomas Hardy, Mrs Gaskell and George Bernard Shaw, as well as painters like Dante Gabriel Rossetti and William Holman Hunt, who portrayed the fallen woman in a sympathetic light, were part of a liberal minority.

Mrs Josephine Butler, the aristocratic wife of a clergyman, was largely responsible for the repeal, after 15 years, of the Contagious Diseases Acts. She was outraged that women should be used for men's satisfaction and then treated as offenders. Her agitation for the repeal of the Acts brought the whole issue out into open and honest discussion. One result was the Criminal Law Amendment Act of 1885, which made both procuring and brothel-keeping illegal – and marked the beginning of the end of widespread prostitution in England. Double standards were to be longer in changing, however, and Samuel Butler's incisive criticisms were to be echoed by several major writers of the 20th century.

disease-ridden – or both – and even the most intrepid reformers never ventured into these areas where crime and violence were a way of life. These prostitutes often supplemented their takings by stealing, since they earned hardly enough to buy gin – and it was among these women that the infamous sex murderer Jack the Ripper found his victims in 1888.

One thing that kept some men 'virtuous' was the fear of venereal disease. It was estimated towards the end of the 19th century that 66 per cent of prostitutes in western Europe had syphilis. The Victorian man was therefore taking a serious risk – if he indulged – of passing on an incurable disease to an innocent wife and to unborn children. One extraordinary example of Victorian attitudes was that for a husband *knowingly and willingly* to infect his wife with venereal disease was not a criminal offence.

Society might turn a blind eye to the habit of visiting prostitutes, but rampant disease was another matter. In an effort to control venereal disease among the armed forces, the Contagious Diseases Acts were passed between 1864 and 1869, which introduced medical check-ups for prostitutes in and around garrison towns.

These Acts aroused a furore. For the first time, prostitution and its consequences were out in the open. Some welcomed the Acts as a practical solution to a major social problem. Others were outraged that the state was seen to condone prostitution, by making it safer, rather than condemning it. Further outrage was caused by the enforcement of the Acts, which permitted the forcible examination of women even suspected of prostitution. Inevitably some women wrongly suspected were subjected to the examination.

Throughout the era there was no shortage of charitable workers and reformers concerned with

Moral reformers
The Reverend Baptist Noel addresses an assembly of 'fallen women' – Victorian ladies of the night. Having gathered them from the streets at midnight, he dangles the carrot of their eternal salvation in the hope of luring them back into the bosom of society.

Poverty and prostitution
For girls born into poverty, life could be unremittingly bleak. Forced to beg for a crust of bread, it was then just a short step to the more lucrative world of prostitution. But the cost was high – syphilis was rampant and a prostitute's life expectancy little more than four years.

BIBLIOGRAPHY

Barnett, Correlli, *Bonaparte*. Hill & Wang (New York, 1978)

Bekker, W.G., *Historical and Critical Review of Samuel Butler's Literary Works* (reprint of 1925 edition). Haskell (Brooklyn, 1969)

Bentley, Joyce, *The Importance of Being Constance: A Biography of Oscar Wilde's Wife*. Beaufort Books (New York, 1984)

Brophy, Brigid, *Black and White: A Portrait of Aubrey Beardsley*. Stein & Day (Briarcliff Manor, 1970)

Carey, John, *Thackeray: Prodigal Genius*. Faber & Faber (Winchester, 1980)

Collins, Phillip, ed., *Thackeray: Interviews and Recollections*, 2 Vols. St Martin's Press (New York, 1983)

De Bremont, Anna, Comtesse, *Oscar Wilde and His Mother* (reprint of 1911 edition). Haskell (Brooklyn, 1972)

De Lange, P. J., *Samuel Butler: Critic and Philosopher* (reprint of 1925 edition). Haskell (Brooklyn, 1969)

Douglas, Alfred, *Oscar Wilde and Myself* (reprint of 1914 edition). Century Bookbindery (Philadelphia, 1983)

Durant, Will and Durant, Ariel, *The Age of Napoleon*. Simon & Schuster (New York, 1975)

Ellmann, Richard, *Oscar Wilde*. Knopf (New York, 1988)

Elton, Oliver, *Dickens and Thackeray*. Porter, Berne (Belfast, 1978)

Farrington, Benjamin, *Samuel Butler and the Odyssey* (reprint of 1929 edition). Arden Library (Darby, 1979)

Festing Jones, Henry, ed., *The Note-Books of Samuel Butler* (reprint of 1915 edition). Richard West (Philadelphia, 1978)

Garnett, Martha R., *Samuel Butler and His Family Relations* (reprint of 1926 edition). Arden Library (Darby, 1980)

Glover, Michael, *The Napoleonic Wars: An Illustrated History 1792-1815*. Hippocrene Books (New York, 1982)

Greenacre, Phyllis, *Quest for the Father: A Study of the Darwin-Butler Controversy*. International Universities Press (New York, 1963)

Hall, N. John, *Trollope and His Illustrators*. St Martin's Press (New York, 1979)

Harden, Edgar F., *Thackeray's "English Humorists."* University of Delaware Press (East Brunswick, 1985)

Hardwick, Michael, *Oscar Wilde*. St Martin's Press (New York, 1985)

Hazen, Charles D., *The French Revolution and Napoleon* (reprint of 1917 edition). Darby Books (Darby, 1982)

Hyde, H. Montgomery, *The Trials of Oscar Wilde*. Dover (New York, 1973)

Kendrick, Walter M., *The Novel Machine: The Theory and Fiction of Anthony Trollope*. Johns Hopkins University Press (Baltimore, 1980)

Kincaid, James R., *The Novels of Anthony Trollope*. Oxford University Press (New York, 1977)

McHugh, Paul, *Prostitution and Victorian Social Reform: The Campaign Against the Contagious Diseases Acts*. St Martin's Press (New York, 1980)

Penelhum, Terence, *Butler*. Routledge & Kegan Paul (Boston, 1985)

Pierrot, Jean, *The Decadent Imagination, 1880-1900*. University of Chicago Press (Chicago, 1984)

Pollard, Arthur, ed., *The Victorians*. Marshall Cavendish (Freeport, 1987)

Steinman, Michael, *Yeat's Heroic Figures: Wilde, Parnell, Swift, Casement*. State University of New York Press (Albany, 1983)

Stephenson, M.F., *The Spiritual Drama in the Life of Thackeray*. Folcroft (Folcroft, 1974)

Super, Robert H., *Trollope in the Post Office*. University of Michigan Press (Ann Arbor, 1981)

Trollope, Anthony, *Thackeray* (reprint of 1887 edition). Folcroft (Folcroft, 1977)

Walkowitz, Judith, *Prostitution and Victorian Society: Women, Class and the State*. Cambridge University Press (New York, 1980)

Wijesinha, Rajiva, *The Androgynous Trollope: Attitudes to Women Amongst Early Victorian Novelists*. University Press of America (Lanham, 1982)

Wilson, James, *Thackeray in the United States* (reprint of 1905 edition). Haskell (Brooklyn, 1970)

INDEX